W9-CLQ-175

# The Seeking Heart

## Fenelon

Volume 4

Library of Spiritual Classics

# The Seeking Heart

## Fenelon

### Including a short biography

**The SeedSowers**
**P.O. Box 3317**
**Jacksonville, FL 32206**
**800.228.2665**
**www.seedsowers.com**

Copyright by Christian Books Publishing House
MCMXCII
Printed in the United States of America
All Rights Reserved

ISBN: 0-940232-49-9
Library of Congress Catalog Card Number: 92-81562

# Acknowledgement

Rewriting a spiritual classic into modern English for today's truth-seeking believer takes incredible time, concentration, effort, and persistence. For these reasons, and for the invaluable aid she has given in producing this book, we express our sincere appreciation to Rose Marie Slosek.

# THE MAN —
# A BIOGRAPHY OF FENELON

The place was the countryside, a few miles outside of the town of Bergerac in the southwestern part of France and in an area called Perigord. On August 6, in the year 1651, Francois de Salignac de La Mothe-Fenelon was born. History remembers him as Francois de Fenelon, or–more simply–Fenelon. At the time of his birth, his father was quite old and, consequently, Fenelon became the major interest of this aging man.*

Until he was twelve years old Fenelon remained at his home receiving a typical Catholic education. He left home at about that age to enroll, for a short time, at the College of Cahors. A major influence entered Fenelon's life at Cahors in the form of his uncle, Marquis Antoine de Fenelon, bishop of Sarlat. His uncle took note of Fenelon's sensitive temperament and the potentiality of this remarkable young boy. Insightfully, his uncle recommended that he transfer to Paris and continue his education there.

In Paris, Fenelon entered the College du Plessis where, soon after, he distinguished himself among his classmates as a scholar possessing an unusual gift of eloquence and speech.

Interestingly, in the years to come, Fenelon's path would cross again and again that of a Catholic priest named Bossuet. There was a similarity in their lives, even in their youth. Like Bossuet, it was at the age of fifteen that Fenelon was allowed to deliver his first sermon. And, like Bossuet,

---

*Fenelon was the second son of the second wife among fifteen children–of Pons de Salignac de Fenelon.

he quickly attracted attention, captivating people by his mannerisms and his scholarship. Fenelon, though, perhaps by the wisdom of his uncle Antoine, was saved from the flattery that was to be the Achilles' heel of Bossuet. And how was the young Fenelon rescued from youthful pride? The Marquis de Fenelon had his young nephew transferred to the Seminary at Saint-Sulpice. (He actually began in a section of the school called the Petit Seminaire.) This occurred in the year 1672 when Fenelon was age 21.

Several major turning points awaited Fenelon at Saint-Sulpice. The first influential factor that moved into his life there was a man named Tronson, director of the seminary. This man was to become Fenelon's closest, dearest friend and counselor.

There was a unique feature to the seminary at Saint-Sulpice. It had a long and very significant relationship to Canada. From Saint-Sulpice a large number of young priests (we would call them missionaries) had gone forth to convert the French portion of the new world. (Remember at that time Eastern Canada was French-speaking.) Soon it was Fenelon's desire to go to this area and take up the cause of this mission. His uncle opposed. Fenelon relented, giving himself over to his studies until the time he was ordained into the priesthood. After his seminary studies were concluded he continued in the parish at Saint-Sulpice.

Fenelon's work was mostly among the poor, the sick and the very sinful. Yet even up until 1675, he had not shaken the idea of the mission field. At that time his ambition was to go to Greece. Again he relinquished this dream, probably in deference to his uncle.

To understand what happened next we need to know a little about the history of France during that period. Ninety percent of France was Catholic, with the other ten percent Protestant, the Protestants being referred to as Huguenots. Under Louis SIV's encouragement, growing persecution was being experienced by the Huguenots.

Some years before, in 1634, a community had been formed in Paris made up of Huguenot women who had left the Protestant faith and joined themselves to the Roman

Catholic church. These Protestants-turned-Catholics were called Nouvelles Catholiques. In about 1678 Fenelon was appointed to head this community. His job was to indoctrinate these women into the Catholic faith and for ten years he devoted himself to this work.

During this period of his life Fenelon developed a close relationship with a few pious friends. One of these close friends was the Duc de Beauvilleiers, a man destined to play a formative role in Fenelon's life.

The Duc's wife was the mother of eight daughters, and Fenelon became something the Catholics called a Spiritual Director, or Spiritual Guide, to this entire family. Out of this experience was to come Fenelon's first book, a work much celebrated in the French world and French language. It is called A Treatise on the Education of Girls.

And now a very dark page in French history opens. In October of 1685, Louis XIV revoked something called The Edict of Nantes (1598) which protected the Protestants of France and gave them a small measure of religious freedom. For several years previous Louis XIV had encouraged increased harassment of the Huguenots. In fact, the reason given for revoking the Edict of Nantes was that there were so few Protestants left in France the law was meaningless. (By no means was this true.)

Persecutions spread. Tens of thousands, and finally hundreds of thousands, of Protestants fled France. Historians have called this perhaps the greatest single blunder ever committed by a reigning monarch in the history of Europe. The Protestants, history would reveal, were the solidifying, cohesive force in the commerce of France. The banking business, accounting, in fact almost the entire financial community and a large part of France's business transactions rested their credibility on the honesty of the Huguenots. When the Huguenots made this exodus from their native land, something of the genius of France disappeared with them.

It was at this time (1685) that the most powerful religious figure in France, Bossuet, recommended that Fenelon be sent to the most troubled area of France, the heavily

Protestant districts of Poitou and Saintogne. Persecution and confusion prevailed there, along with an air of rebellion. The king, who virtually always did whatever Bossuet suggested in religious matters, dispatched Fenelon to this area. Fenelon agreed, with one rather unusual stipulation. He was not to be accompanied by military troops, but rather, he would go to do a work of peace and mercy. It was a task he was well equipped for by his nature and by the experience afforded him with the Nouvelles Catholiques in Paris. The military was to withdraw from any area where Fenelon had jurisdiction.

Fenelon understood the Protestant mind.

A story illustrates how this man wove his way through the impossible situation in Saintogne. A devout Catholic called upon Fenelon to come attend to his kin, a dying Protestant "heretic." On the way, Fenelon composed a prayer which, we are told, the two men–a Protestant heretic and a Catholic bishop–prayed together!

*"Thou knowest, my Savior, that I desire to live and die in the Truth; forgive me if I was mistaken."*

As his stay in this area lengthened, both the Huguenots and the Catholics were impressed with the way he handled his task. It was said that though the Protestants were not converted by him they were charmed by his character. Grudgingly, perhaps, it seems he may have even won their esteem and admiration. Fenelon's success in Poitou caused the public, for the first time, to focus attention upon this man and his ministry.

In August 1689, when Fenelon was 38, he was given one of the most influential positions that could befall any Frenchman. Louis appointed him Preceptor of the Duc of Burgundy. That title may have very little meaning to anyone unacquainted with French history. But we understand the implication better when we realize that, for all practical purposes, Fenelon was given the task of raising the young man who would succeed Louis XIV to the throne of France. Fenelon was now in the inner circle of influence in France. He also had one of the most difficult tasks imagin-

iv

able, as the young Duc was a terror. Could Fenelon handle him?

A contemporary of Fenelon has left us the following description of Fenelon's appearance. Reading it helps us to understand a little better the magnetism of this man.

"This prelate was a tall, thin man, well made, pale, with a large nose, eyes from whence fire and talents streamed as from a torrent, a physiognomy the like of which I have never seen in any other man, and which, once seen, one could never forget. He combined everything, and the greatest contradictions produce no want of harmony. A united seriousness and gaiety, gravity and courtesy, the man of learning, the bishop and the grand seigneur; the prevailing characteristics, as in everything about him, being refinement, intellect, gracefulness, modesty, and above all, noblesse.

"It was difficult to take one's eyes off of him. He possessed a natural eloquence, grace and finesse, and a most insinuating, yet noble and appropriate courtesy; an easy, clear, agreeable utterance; a wonderful power of explaining the hardest matter in a lucid, distinct manner. He was a man who never sought to seem cleverer than those with whom he conversed, who brought himself insensibly to their level, putting them at their ease, and enthralling them so, one could neither leave him, nor mistrust him, nor help seeking him again."

Another contemporary describes Fenelon this way:

"...one of those rare men, destined to create an epoch in their times, and to do honor as much to humanity by their virtue as to letters by their exceeding talent,—easy, brilliant, characterized by fertile, graceful, dominant imagination, which yet never made its domination felt. His eloquence was winning rather than vehement, and he reigned as much through the charm he had on society as by

*the superiority of his talents; always bringing
himself to the level of others, and never arguing;
seeming, on the contrary, to yield to others at the
very time he was convincing them. His whole
bearing was marked with a noble singularity, and
an indescribable and sublime simplicity gave a
sort of prophet-like stamp to his character; the
fresh, though unaffected, way in which he expressed himself made many people fancy that he
knew everything by inspiration. He seemed almost
as if he had invented rather than acquired the
sciences. He was always original, always cre-
ative, imitating no one, and himself wholly in-
imitable."*

It has been said of him that he was a man dead to vanity.
One of his contemporaries noted, "I never knew him to
speak brusquely to anyone, nor to the best of my knowledge
did a harsh or contemptuous word ever escape him." Yet
another observer gave this critique of Fenelon.

*"I have seen him adapt himself within a short
space of time to all classes,—associating with the
great and using their style, without any loss of
episcopal dignity, and then turning to the lowly
and young, like a kind father teaching his children.
There was no effort or affection in his readiness to
turn from one to the other; it seemed as though his
mind naturally embraced all varieties."*

It was to this man that was given the Herculean task of
bringing a violent and difficult seven-year-old child into
management. But just how difficult was this child? Here is a
description left to us of the little monster!

*"Monseigneur was born with the disposition
which made one tremble. He was so passionate
that he would break the clocks when they struck the
hour which summoned him to some unwelcomed
duty, and fly into the wildest rage at the rain which
hindered some pleasure. Resistance made him*

vi

*perfectly furious. I have often been a witness to this in his early childhood. Moreover, a strong inclination attached him to whatever was forbidden to his mind or body. His satirical power was all the more biting because it was clever and pungent, and he seized promptly on the ridiculous side of things. He gave himself up to all that pleased him with a violent passion, and with an amount of pride and hauteur past description; he was dangerously quick in penetrating both things and people, in seeing the weak side, and reasoning more powerfully and deeply than his masters. But on the other hand, as soon as the storm of passion was over, reason would return and get the upper hand; he would see his faults and acknowledge them, sometimes so regretfully as almost to renew the storm. His mind was lively, quick, penetrating, resolute to meet difficulty...literally speaking, transcendent in every way. The marvel is that in so short a time devotion and grace should have made an altogether new being of him and changed so many redoubtable faults into the entirely opposite virtues."*

And here is another description of the young man who, save for the miracle called Fenelon, was destined to be a tyrant.

*"He was intensely obstinate, desperately fond of good eating, of hunting, of music, of games at which it was dangerous to play, and he could not endure to be beaten; he was disposed to be cruel, and he looked upon the rest of mankind as an inferior race with which he had nothing in common. Even his brothers, who were supposed to be brought up on precisely the same footing as himself, he considered as merely a sort of link between himself and the ordinary human race."*

And so Fenelon set about his task. He was to give the child a literary education, but his main struggle was the boy's fiery temperament. It was patience and gentleness together with firmness that began to corral the fury of this wild child who would be king.

When one of his evil moods seized him, instructions were given to everyone in the household to relapse into silence. No one was to speak to him if they could help it. He was to be treated with a sort of humiliating compassion which might be shown a madman; his books and everything else that had to do with the constructive part of his life were to be put aside as useless in this state of rage.

This tactic had a gradual effect upon the young boy. Full of penitence, he would sometimes come and throw himself in the fullest affection and trust, mixed with childish remorse, upon the never-failing patience of his Preceptor. A bond grew between them. Soon the boy was won over to Fenelon and continued to almost worship him until the very day he died. He even grew to learn to assist those who strove to conquer his faults.

It was the ensuing three years that he lived in the court of Louis XIV that Fenelon wrote two more works, *The Dialogue of Death, and Telemaque.* (*Telemaque* ranks in French literature something like one of Shakespeare's better works might in English literature. Its content has caused some to call Fenelon "the first modern mind.") Also during this same period the single greatest influence of his adult life was to make its entrance. While in the king's court, Fenelon met Jeanne Guyon. She, in turn, was to introduce Fenelon to a deeper relationship with Jesus Christ. It is to the everlasting credit of this powerful and influential man that he humbled himself before this obscure woman and received from her the guidance that he did.

But don't expect a secular historian to agree with that observation! Secular historians have never forgiven Guyon for being the one flaw in Fenelon's life, causing him to be denied a cardinal's cap and a place in French history alongside the very greatest of her sons.

Events begin to move quickly now. Fenelon is caring for the grandson of the king, the honors of the world and the admiration of France are upon him. In 1693 he is chosen to become a member of the French academy. The next year, in appreciation for what Fenelon had done for his grandson, Louis XIV gave Fenelon the position of Abbey of Saint Valery. One year later, in 1695, the Pope elevated Fenelon to the auspicious position of Archbishop of an area in France called Cambrai. (An Archbishop is one step from Cardinal, which is but one step from Pope!)

But in exactly those same years, Bossuet made himself the enemy of Jeanne Guyon. Now it happened that the two most powerful religious figures in France found themselves on a collision course. Fenelon was Guyon's friend; Bossuet was her avowed enemy.

Fenelon could find nothing wrong with either Guyon's life or her teachings. He even went further to become her defender, knowing full well the danger of crossing the powerful Bossuet.

At the same time, in their private lives, both men were working on a book, neither knowing the other was doing so. Bossuet, knowing nothing of Fenelon's book, asked Fenelon to endorse his own. The book by Bossuet condemned the teachings of Jeanne Guyon, and Fenelon refused. Bossuet was outraged. Bossuet soon found not only the teaching of Jeanne Guyon unacceptable, but also Fenelon's book *The Maxims of the Saints* just as bad. Bossuet was determined to cross swords with his friend Fenelon and ruin him in the battle. So ensued one of the greatest ecclesiastical confrontations that church history has ever recorded.

Bossuet published a book accusing Fenelon of holding doctrines contrary to the true faith and called upon Fenelon to make response. Fenelon wrote a short book to his defense. Bossuet wrote a book denouncing Fenelon, his teachings and his answer. Each answered with another book and after that, each answered the answer with yet another book! Paris (as well as France and a good part of Europe) was standing on its ear. This series of books, from the hands of these two awesome men, were literally the talk of a large portion of the continent. These little books are still considered to be literary masterpieces. The only way to adequately describe the place this confrontation holds in

French history would be to compare it to the Lincoln-Douglas debates in the United States. (If you are British, try to imagine a literary duel between Shakespeare and John Locke.) Until this very day, the school children of France study this clash of titans both in their French history classes and in French literature.

Louis XIV, siding with Bossuet–as always–forbade Fenelon to live any longer in Paris and removed him as Preceptor of his grandson. The controversy spiraled.

Bossuet demanded that Fenelon be investigated. The whole matter landed on the desk of the Pope himself, the same Pope who had only recently purged himself of the Michael Molinos dispute!*

A Vatican committee was appointed to settle the matter. It took that committee years to thrash through the matter. Bossuet threw the totality of his influence behind a demand for the worst possible condemnation and in so doing tarnished his place in history. The final verdict handed down by the committee was not much more than a hand-slap on Fenelon. Bossuet was outraged. The original book, *The Maxims of the Saints*, was only moderately condemned. The final written statement on the matter was a study in mildness of condemnation. The Pope showed the greatest tenderness and respect for Fenelon. Nonetheless, Fenelon's book had been denounced and, upon receiving word of this Fenelon immediately recanted. (In Roman Catholic circles, this simply means that he renounced his own teachings.) He did this out of firm belief that he was to be submissive to the Pope and to the mother church in all things.

Although he was allowed to remain Archbishop, Fenelon was banished to his diocese.

In the meantime, Bossuet and Louis XIV had seen to it that Guyon had been imprisoned, without trial and without even charges being laid against her. The influence of Jeanne Guyon on the court of Louis XIV and even upon the religious life of France had come to an end. Nonetheless,

---

*See* The Spiritual Guide, *also published by* The SeedSowers.

the things she said, the things she stood for and the testimony of her life have had a habit of periodically resurrecting now and again. For better or worse, Guyon has simply never "quietly gone away."

The now-banished Fenelon devoted the remainder of his life to the duties of his diocese. It was during this time he penned most of the letters you will find in this book.

Unfortunately, few of his sermons have been left to us. The writings for which he is mostly remembered are *The Maxims of the Saints*, *Telemaque*, and his letters. (His works on child raising are all but forgotten, yet their concepts are, to this very hour, woven into the fabric of western culture.)

His letters are generally conceded to be the most perfect of their kind to be found in the French language. Many a believer has found solace and benefit in his thoughtful correspondence. They are, truly, spiritual letters and some of the best Christian correspondence dealing with the matter of a deeper walk with Christ which has ever found its way to print.

What was not learned about Fenelon until the twentieth century was that, even years after Jeanne Guyon was released from prison, the two of them carried on a secret correspondence. Here is clear evidence that neither of them really abandoned either the belief or practice of their walk with the Lord.

It is interesting to note that the three great Catholic names of this era (as deals with the deeper aspects of the faith)—Molinos, Guyon and Fenelon—held on to their convictions to the very end of their lives.

Perhaps the greatest disappointment to come to Fenelon and Guyon was the death of the king's grandson in 1712. They had hoped this young man would succeed Louis XIV and bring to France a real witness of Jesus Christ and perhaps, they dreamed, that he might play a major role in the reformation of the Catholic Church. The young Duc's death was, in fact, a moment of sadness that stilled the hopes of an entire nation.

Two years later Fenelon suffered another keen loss.

Fenelon's friend, the Duc du Beauvilleiers, died in 1714. Fenelon was broken hearted, not realizing that he himself had only four more months to live, for, by that time, Fenelon's own health had broken.

In November of 1714, while crossing a bridge, one of the horses pulling his carriage shied...the carriage overturned, and Fenelon was injured. He came down with fever on January 1, 1715. By the end of the week, on January 7 at 5:15 in the morning, Fenelon passed away at the age of 63.

Two years later Jeanne Guyon, who was two years older than he, also died. An epoch in French history had ended. A high water mark in Christian devotion and in experiential faith was over, yet their influence seems to have a disconcerting way of rising from the dead from time to time. Perhaps we live in such a day.

# The
# Seeking
# Heart

# Part I

## The Way of the Cross

# EMBRACING THE CROSS

You need to learn to separate yourself from unnecessary and restless thoughts which grow out of self-love. When your own thoughts are set aside you will be completely in the middle of the straight and narrow path. You will experience the freedom and peace that is meant for you as a child of God.

I try to follow the same advice that I give others. I know that I must seek peace in the same way. Often, when you suffer, it is the life of your self-nature that causes you pain. When you are dead you do not suffer. If you were completely dead to your old nature you would no longer feel many of the pains that now bother you.

Endure the aches and pains of your body with patience. Do the same thing with your spiritual afflictions (that is, trouble sent to you that you cannot control). Do not add to the cross in your life by becoming so busy that you have no time to sit quietly before God. Do not resist what God brings into your life. Be willing to suffer if that is what is needed. Overactivity and stubbornness will only increase your anguish.

God prepares a cross for you that you must embrace without thought of self-preservation. The cross is painful. Accept the cross and you will find peace even in the middle of turmoil. Let me warn you that if you push the cross away, your circumstances will become twice as hard to bear. In the long run, the pain of resisting the cross is harder to live with than the cross itself.

See God's hand in the circumstances of your life. Do you want to experience true happiness? Submit yourself peacefully and simply to the will of God, and bear your sufferings without struggle. Nothing so shortens and soothes your pain as the spirit of non-resistance to your Lord.

As wonderful as this sounds, it still may not stop you from bargaining with God. The hardest thing about suffering is not knowing how great it will be or how long it will last. You will be tempted to want to impose some limits to your suffering. No doubt you will want to control the intensity of your pain.

Do you see the stubborn and hidden hold you have over your life? This control makes the cross necessary in the first place. Do not reject the full work that the power of the cross could accomplish in you. Unfortunately, you will be forced to go over the same ground again and again. Worse yet, you will suffer much, but your suffering will be for no purpose.

May the Lord deliver you from falling into an inner state in which the cross is not at work in you! God loves a cheerful giver. (II Corinthians 9:7) Imagine how much He must love those who abandon themselves to His will cheerfully and completely—even if it results in their crucifixion!

# SURRENDER
# TO HIS PLANS

I am truly sorry about all your troubles, but I know that God is working on your behalf. Remember that God loves you and therefore He does not spare you! He lays on you the cross of Jesus Christ. Whatever revelations you receive or whatever emotional experiences you have are worthless unless they lead you to the very real and constant practice of dying to your self-nature. Unfortunately, you cannot die without suffering, nor can you be said to be fully dead while part of you still lives.

The death that God brings you will pierce deep within. Soul and spirit will be divided. He sees in you all that you cannot see. He knows exactly where the fatal blows should fall. He heads straight for that which you are most reluctant to give up. Pain is only felt where there is life. And in this situation life is precisely the place where death is needed.

Your Father wastes no time by cutting into that which is already dead. If He wanted to let you remain as you are, He would certainly do so. He seeks to destroy your old nature. He can only accomplish this by cutting into that which is alive. Do not expect Him to attack only those obviously wicked desires which you renounced forever when you gave yourself to Him. Rather, He may test you be taking away the wonderful sense of freedom you feel, or by taking from you all that now brings you spiritual comfort.

Will you resist? No! Allow everything! Volunteer for your own death, for God will only accomplish His work to the extent that you let Him. Do not push away the progress that God wants to make in your life.

Cheerfully give up everything you now rely on to God's good pleasure. Give up spiritual things, too, whenever He wants to take them from you. What do you fear, you of little faith? Are you afraid that He may not be able to give you His strength when He takes away yours? Why does He take it away? Only so that He might be your supply. The lesson may be painful, but He wishes to purify you. I see that every natural means of help is shut off. God intends to accomplish His work in you by cutting off every human resource. He is a jealous God. He wants you to see that what He is going to do within you can only be done by Himself alone.

Surrender to His plans. Allow yourself to be led where He wants to take you. Be careful when you seek help from people when God is not wanting you to. Remember that they can only give you what He gives to them to give you. Why should it bother you that you can no longer drink from the faucet? You are now being led to drink from the ever-flowing spring!

# THE BENEFIT OF TRIALS

You have some difficult trials to bear but you need them since God has allowed these events to happen. He knows how to select them. You could not have picked for yourself what God brings into your life through the cross. The cross that you would pick out would build your self-will instead of breaking it down.

There are times when everything in life seems to be a trial. Sometimes there is only suffering. Still, the heaviest cross must be carried in peace. Sometimes the cross can neither be carried or dragged. Then you can only fall down beneath it, overwhelmed and exhausted. I pray that God may spare you from suffering as much as possible.

Remember that God is not unaware of your suffering. He allows your suffering. See that He alone knows what is best for you. Live by faith as you embrace your trials. Confidently trust in God, even when you do not see what He is doing. Trust that God, with great compassion, gives you trials in proportion to the help that He wants to bring to you. There is no doubt that the life of faith is the most penetrating of all deaths.

You complain about your inward darkness and poverty of spirit. Jesus says, "Blessed are the poor in spirit." It is good for you to see your weakness, but don't excuse it. Remain simple and low before God and He will bring you peace, gentleness, longsuffering, and contentment even in your trouble.

# THE CROSS—
# A BOND OF LOVE

I am sorry to hear of your troubles, but I am sure you realize that you must carry the cross with Christ in this life. Soon enough there will come a time when you will no longer suffer. You will reign with God and He will wipe away your tears with His own hand. In His presence, pain and sighing will forever flee away.

So while you have the opportunity to experience difficult trials, do not lose the slightest opportunity to embrace the cross. Learn to suffer in humility and in peace. Your deep self-love makes the cross too heavy to bear. Learn to suffer with simplicity and a heart full of love. If you do you will not only be happy in spite of the cross, but because of it. Love is pleased to suffer for the Well-Beloved. The cross which conforms you into His image is a consoling bond of love between you and Him.

# TRUST YOUR SELF-LOVE
# TO GOD

I have no doubt that God treats you as one of His friends by giving you the cross. God's way accomplishes His purpose quicker than anything you could think of. God is able to seek out and destroy the roots of self-love. You, on your own, could never find those hidden roots. God can see the entire path of self-love within your heart. Let Him attack self-love at its strongest point.

Pray for strength and faith enough to trust yourself completely to God. Follow Him simply wherever He may lead you and you will not have to think up big plans to bring about your perfection. Your new life will begin to grow naturally.

I know you want to see the road ahead rather than trusting God. If you continue this way, the road will get longer and your spiritual progress will slow down. Give yourself as completely as you can to God. Do so until your final breath, and He will never desert you.

# THE PATH OF CHRIST

God will eventually test you in all areas of your life, but He will not let your trials become greater than you can bear. Let God use trials to help you grow. Do not try to measure your progress, your strength, or what God is doing. His work is not less efficient because what He is doing is invisible. Much of God's work is done in secret because you would not die to yourself if He always visibly stretched out His hand to save you. God does not transform you on a bed of light, life, and grace. His transformation is done on the cross in darkness, poverty, and death.

What valid questions do you have about the truth of Christianity? You really fear having to submit to someone beside yourself. You also fear having to walk the difficult road toward becoming conformed to the image of Christ. You see clearly the sacrifices you will have to make to follow Christ completely and you are shrinking back.

Christ did not say, "If anyone will come after me, let him enjoy himself, let him be gorgeously dressed, let him be drunk with delight." He never even said, "Be glad that you are perfect and that you can see how well you are doing." No, Jesus said, "If anyone will come after me, let him deny himself, take up his cross and follow me." His path winds up the side of a steep mountain where death will be present on every hand. (Matthew 16:24)

You do not yet see the lovely side of following Christ. You see what He takes away, but you do not see what He gives. You exaggerate the sacrifices and ignore the blessings.

Paul tells you that you desire to be clothed, but it is necessary that you be stripped before you can put on Christ. Allow Him to strip your self-love of every covering so that you might receive the white robe washed in the blood of the Lamb. You need only His purity.

Listen to what I have to say. It is not easy to hear, but it will feed your spirit. Do not listen to the voice that suggests that you live for yourself. The voice of self-love is even more powerful than the voice of the serpent. If the world never asked for anything more than what you could give out of love, wouldn't it be a better master?

Christ leaves no emptiness within you. You will be led to do things which you will find enjoyable, and you will like them better than doing all the things which have led you astray. How happy you will be when you do not possess anything of your own but give yourself completely to your Lord. Bride of Jesus, how beautiful you are when you no longer have anything of your own, but seek only His beauty. You will then be the delight of your Bridegroom, and He will be all your beauty! He will love you without measure. He will put His own life in you.

# DIE DAILY

Many think that "dying to themselves" is what causes them so much pain. But it is actually part of them that still lives that causes the problem. Death is only painful to you when you resist it. Your imagination exaggerates how bad death will be. Self-love fights with all of its strength to live. Die inwardly as well as outwardly. Let all that is not born of God within you die.

Bear your cross. Do you know what this means? Learn to see yourself as you are, and accept your weakness until it pleases God to heal you. Your goal is to be as patient with yourself as you are with your neighbor. If you die a little bit every day of your life, you won't have too much to worry about on your final day. Self-love brings great anxiety. No wonder you worry about the future so much. Be patient with yourself and allow your fellow Christians to help you. How completely will these daily deaths destroy the power of your final dying. Then your bodily death will be but a falling asleep. Happy are you who sleep this sleep of peace!

# DIFFICULT
# CIRCUMSTANCES

God doesn't want to discourage you or to spoil you. Embrace the difficult circumstances you find yourself in—even when you feel they will overwhelm you. Allow God to mold you through the events He allows to enter your life. This will make you flexible toward the will of God. The events of life are like a furnace for the heart. All your impurities are melted and your old ways are lost.

As for the humiliation you feel when you see your faults—simply see how sensitive your self-love is. The pain you feel at your own imperfection is worse than the faults themselves. Your problem really is that you become so irritated by seeing your faults. Learn to live with yourself as you really are without being so upset. If you do this, you will soon have peace.

Patiently endure the ups and downs of everyday life. Behind every annoying circumstance, learn to see God governing all things. See that He trains you through troubling situations as well as through pleasant ones. The intrusions that God sends you will no doubt upset your plans and oppose all that you want. But they will also chase you toward God. Sit still before Him and yield your will to Him. Your unbending will shall begin to learn flexibility.

Everything that comes from God's hand produces good fruit. Sometimes the annoyances that make you long for solitude are better for producing humility than the most complete solitude could be. Use the circumstances of each moment to the fullest. Sometimes an exciting book, or an inspiring devotional time, or a deep conversation about spiritual matters will make you feel extremely satisfied with yourself. You will believe that you are farther along than you really are. Talking about the cross is not at all the same as experiencing it. So remember this: Do not seek annoying circumstances, but when they come bear them in peace. It is easy to delude yourself! Do not seek God as if He were far off in an ivory castle. He is found in the middle of the events of your everyday life. Look past the obstacles and find Him.

# THE WAYS OF GOD

When God starts to deal with your old nature He heads straight for the center of all that you hold most dear. Allow Him to bring you the cross in the very center of who you are. Don't grumble and become agitated when the process starts: Silence and peace will help you much more than being upset.

You will be tempted to speak out in a humble tone of voice to tell others of your problems. Watch out for this! A humility that is still talkative does not run very deep. When you talk too much your self-love relieves its sense of shame a little.

Don't be angry about what people say. Just follow God and let them talk. As far as people are concerned, you will never be able to satisfy them. Silence, peace, and union with God should comfort you from all that people speak against you. You need to be determined to do right in your present situation—but at the same time your quick temper requires checks and balances. Come to God often just to sit in His presence and renew yourself. Nothing is as important as lowliness of heart, and detachment from your own opinion and will. Stiffness and harshness is not the spirit of Jesus Christ.

# TAKE UP YOUR CROSS

To bear the cross simply, without letting your self-love add all sorts of dilemmas to it, will make your life easier. When you accept the cross and simply allow it to do the work God intended, you will be happy because you will see what good fruit is produced in you.

When you love God, it will not matter to you what you must suffer on His behalf. The cross will make you over in the image of your Beloved. Here is real consolation—a true bond of love.

You are bearing the burden of some old ones who can no longer bear their own. Reason weakens at so old an age. Goodness, unless deeply rooted, lessens. All the strength seems to go to the temper! Accept and welcome this burden as the cross.

It is a blessing that you have some free hours to rest in peace in the bosom of the Lord. This is where you will refresh yourself and gain strength to go on. Take care of your health and try to take some time to rest and enjoy yourself. As others grow older you should expect less and less of them. Don't expect too much of yourself, either.

# TEMPER YOUR STANDARDS

Suffering is necessary for all of us. You will be purified by dying to your own desires and will. Let yourself die! You have excellent opportunities for this to happen—don't waste them!

I agree that the daily standards that you live by should not be relaxed in any way. Yet you must deal gently with the faults of others. Learn to be lenient with the less important matters, but maintain your firmness over that which is essential.

Remember that true firmness is gentle, humble, and calm. A sharp tongue, a proud heart, and an iron hand have no place in God's work. Wisdom "sweetly orders all things." Do you act this way? If you ever find yourself acting otherwise, humble yourself immediately. Uphold a godly standard, but admit when you uphold it in an ungodly way.

No book or prayer will help you die to yourself as much as facing the humiliation of your daily failures. Of course you must still retire inwardly and be faithful to bring yourself before God. I also warn you not to let your business distract you from your spiritual life. If you allow yourself to be constantly distracted, your heart will grow hard. Retire to pray when you can and live the rest of your day in love.

# UPS AND DOWNS

Let the ups and downs of your spiritual life come and go. If you were always down, you would become hardened and discouraged. God gives you seasons when you can catch your breath.

Let me tell you about myself. When I suffer, I can never see an end to my trials. And when relief comes, I am so suspicious that the suffering is not really over that I hesitate to accept my rest. It seems to me that to accept both "good" and "bad" seasons alike is to be truly fruitful. Accept both comfort and correction from the hand of God.

Of course, this is all very easy for me to say to you, but I want you to know that I cringe at the very thought of the cross coming to work in me. I am not telling you that experiencing the cross will be easy. Outwardly it will be difficult, but inwardly it can be worse—a time of agony and dryness. If I sound a bit pessimistic, it is because I am writing to you in the midst of a spiritual dry spell. I don't know what tomorrow brings. God will do what seems good to Him. Sometimes what He wants is hard to accept. Listen to God—there is true freedom, peace, and joy in Him.

# BEARING AFFLICTION

I am sorry that one near to you is an invalid. Encourage her not to distrust God. He will give her patience to bear with her suffering. Only God knows what her limit is. Neither you nor she know the limits of her strength, or how long this trial will continue. Understandably, this can lead to discouragement.

"God is faithful and will not allow you to be tempted above what you are able to bear." He pledges His faithfulness and how wonderful is this faithfulness!

Remind your friend of this and tell her to leave everything in God's hands without looking at tomorrow. Often that which you imagine to be so terrible and unbearable is not so bad when it actually happens. Your imagination makes things harder on you than God ever could. You want to know the future and you also exaggerate your suffering. Sometimes you become overwhelmed by events that have not yet happened. All moments are in God's hands. Walk humbly with God.

# THE BONDAGE OF SELF

Chains of gold can become like chains of iron. And while people envy you while you wear fine jewelry, you can become the prisoner of such finery. Your bondage is no better than the person who is unjustly kept prison. The only comfort you have is that God, in His wisdom, has allowed this, and this is the same comfort that an innocent prisoner has.

The comfort that comes from knowing you are in God's hands in inexhaustible. When you are in God's care nothing else matters. How blessed you are when you are cut off from your own will so that you might follow God's will. But it is no easy journey! Let me tell you what it is like: You can no longer live for yourself. Day and night you do only what God wants. But so much the better! He keeps you bound hand and foot and never leaves you a moment to yourself! Shall I go on? He leads you to sacrifice more and more, and you go from one troublesome situation to another! He trains you to fulfill His noble plans amidst the petty annoyances and aggravations of life. And He doesn't allow you much more than a moment's rest! Hardly will one annoying person have gone before God sends another to you.

You think that it is spiritually important to have free time to be alone with God; but I tell you, you will really get closer to Him by embracing the cross in your life, and not always seeking to experience tender moments in the presence of God. When the torrential floods of daily business sweep you away, just let yourself be carried off with no regret. Don't you know you will find God in this torrent, too?

Jesus said to Peter, "Before, you walked where you wanted to, but when you are older, another stronger than you will guide you and lead you to where you do not want to go." Like Peter, let yourself be led in this way. To dream of freedom is a lovely idea, but perhaps you will never reach it. You need to realize that you might die in your present condition. The Israelites in Babylon longed for Jerusalem, but there were many who never saw Jerusalem, and died in Babylon. What if those people had waited until they got to Jerusalem to serve God? Be like those Israelites who served God even in captivity.

# THE HIDDEN CROSS

God has all sorts of circumstances to bring you the cross, and they all accomplish His purpose. He may even join physical weakness to your emotional and spiritual suffering. Of course the world may not see you dealing with the cross—they think you are just touchy or prone to fits of nervous exhaustion. So while you are bent double under the hidden work of the cross, onlookers often envy your apparent good fortune.

What do you say to God when you are under the work of the cross? You need not say a lot to Him, or even think of Him much. He sees your suffering, and your willingness to submit. With people you love you do not need to continually say, "I love you with all my heart." Even if you do not think about how much you love Him, you still love God every bit as much. True love is deep down in the spirit—simple, peaceful, and silent.

How do you bear suffering? Silently before God. Do not disturb yourself by trying to manufacture an artificial sense of God's presence. Slowly you will learn that all the troubles in your life—your job, your health, your inward failings—are really cures to the poison of your old nature. Learn to bear these sufferings in patience and meekness.

# THE NATURE OF
# SELF-DENIAL

Self-denial has its place in a Christian's life, but God doesn't ask you to choose what is most painful to you. If you followed this path you would soon ruin your health, reputation, business, and friendship.

Self-denial consists of bearing patiently all those things that God allows to pass into your life. If you don't refuse anything that comes in God's order, you are tasting of the cross of Jesus Christ.

God gives you grace to bear the cross in your life just like He provides for your daily bread. He will never fail you! It is a good exercise for over-enthusiastic people to give up their own ways of practicing self-denial, and to allow God to bring whatever He will into their lives.

If you are not willing to accept the self-denials appointed by God, then don't trust the self-denials that you come up with. Examine what you are doing. Trust God to bring you what you need.

# THE VALUE OF
# THE CROSS

Do you wonder why God has to make it so hard on you? Why doesn't He make you good without making you miserable in the meantime? Of course He could, but He does not choose to do so. He wants you to grow a little at a time and not burst into instant maturity. This is what He has decided and you can only adore His wisdom—even when you don't understand it.

I am awed by what suffering can produce. You and I are nothing without the cross. I agonize and cry when the cross is working within me, but when it is over I look back in admiration for what God has accomplished. Of course I am then ashamed that I bore it so poorly. I have learned so much from my foolish reactions.

You yourself must endure the painful process of change. There is much more at work here than your instant maturity. God wants to build a relationship with you that is based on faith and trust and not on glamorous miracles.

God uses the disappointments, disillusionments, and failures of your life to take your trust away from yourself and help you put your trust in Him. It is like being burned in a slow fire, but you would rather be burned up in a blaze of glory, wouldn't you? How would this fast burn detach you from yourself? Thus God prepares events to detach you from yourself and from others.

God is your Father, do you think He would ever hurt you? He just cuts you off from those things you love in the wrong way. You cry like a baby when God removes something or someone from your life, but you would cry a lot more if you saw the eternal harm your wrong attachments cause you.

You do not see with the eyes of eternity. God knows everything. Nothing happens without His consent. You are upset by small losses, but do not see eternal gains! Don't dwell on your suffering. Your oversensitivity makes your trials worse. Abandon yourself to God.

Everything in you that is not already a part of the established kingdom of God needs the cross. When you accept the cross in love, His kingdom begins to come to life within you. You must bear the cross and be satisfied with what pleases God. You have need of the cross. The faithful Giver of every good gift gives the cross to you with His own hand. I pray you will come to see how blessed it is to be corrected for your own good.

My God, help us to see Jesus as our model in all suffering. You nailed Him to the cross for us. You made Him a man of sorrows to teach us how useful sorrow is. Give us a heart to turn our backs on ourselves and trust only in You.

# A VIOLENT KINGDOM

Whom do you think Paul was talking to when he said, "We are fools for the sake of Jesus Christ, and you are wise in Jesus Christ." To you! Not to the people who do not know God! He is talking to all who think they can work out their own salvation without accepting the folly of the cross of Jesus. No one wants to be humiliated and put down. It is not something to be excited about, but it is the way of God.

You cannot give place to the world, to your passions or your laziness. Words are not enough to claim the kingdom of God. It takes strength and courage and violence. You must violently resist the tides of the world. Violently give up all that holds you back from God. Violently turn your will over to God to do His will alone.

This violence is what I pray you will come to know, for how else will you know anything of the life of the Lord Jesus?

# HUMILIATION

The most important thing is humility. Humility gives you a teachable spirit that makes everything easier. Consider the life of Jesus. He was born in a stable. He had to flee to Egypt. He worked thirty years in the shop of a craftsman. He suffered hunger, thirst, and fatigue. He was poor and He was ridiculed. He taught the doctrine of heaven and no one listened to Him. He was treated like a slave, betrayed, and died between two thieves.

Jesus' life was full of humiliation, but we are horrified by the slightest humiliation. How do you expect to know Jesus if you do not seek Him where He was found: in suffering and the cross? You must imitate Him. But don't think you can follow Him in your own strength—you are going to have to find all your strength in Him. Remember that Jesus wants to feel all your weaknesses.

Seek to follow Jesus along the road of humility that He has taken. The greatest profit which you can gather from an experience of your weakness is to let your frailties help you become more humble and obedient.

# THE SACRIFICE OF LOVE

If you follow God only to feel His presence and comfort, then you follow Him for the wrong reasons. Your mind is anxious to know, your heart wants to feel sweet feelings, but you are not willing to follow Christ to the cross. Is this dying to self?

There is refined spiritual ambition in unduly pursuing spiritual gifts. Paul speaks of a better way. "Love does not seek her own." How will you go on to maturity if you are always seeking the consolation of feeling the presence of God with you? To seek pleasure and to ignore the cross will not get you very far. You will soon be trapped in the pursuit of spiritual pleasures.

If you have too tender a childhood in Jesus Christ, you will be in for a hard time when God starts to wean you away from the sensed comfort of God's presence. Don't live on the porch and think you are in the house! The beginnings of your faith may be accompanied by many wonderful feelings, but this does not mean you are mature. Hold to God alone and do not rely on anything you feel or taste or imagine. You will come to see how much safer this way is than chasing after visions and prophesies.

# THE PURPOSE OF
# SUFFERING

God never makes you suffer unnecessarily. He intends for your suffering to heal and purify you. The hand of God hurts you as little as it can.

Anxiety brings suffering. Sometimes you are simply unwilling to suffer, and you end up resisting God's work. If you put away all your restless longings and your anxiety, you will experience the peace and freedom that God gives to His children. The yoke that God gives is easy to bear if you accept it without struggling to escape. You make life more painful for yourself when you resist God in the least way.

Usually you bargain with God to set a limit on your suffering. The same inward waywardness that makes the work of the cross necessary in your life is what will try to push the cross away. God has to start over with you every time you push Him away.

Sometimes God takes away His gifts until you can possess them purely. Otherwise, they will poison you. It is rare to hold God's gifts without possessiveness. You think everything is for you. You do not think first of the glory of God or you would not become depressed when your visible blessings vanish. The truth is, you are mostly concerned with yourself. Self-love is proud of its spiritual accomplishments. You must lose everything to find God for Himself alone. But you won't lose everything until it is ripped from you. You won't begin to let go of yourself until you have been thrown off a cliff! He takes away to give back in a better way.

Look at the example of friendships. At first God attracts you by pouring His presence out on you. You are eager to pray and to turn away from your selfish comforts and friendships. You give up everyone and everything that does not feel the same as you do. Many people never get past this place. Some get past this to letting God strip them of everything, but get depressed when everything becomes a burden. Far from looking for friends, the friends they used to enjoy now irritate them. Here is agony and despair. Joy cannot be found.

Does this surprise you? God takes everything because you do not know how to love, so do not speak of friendship. The very idea brings tears to your eyes. Everything overcomes you. You do not know what you want. You are moody and cry like a child. You are a mass of swirling emotions which change from moment to moment. Do you find it hard to believe that a strong and high-minded person can be reduced to such a state? To speak of friendship is like speaking of dancing to a sick person.

Wait until the winter is past. Your true friends will come back to you. You will no longer love for yourself, but in and for God. Before, you were somehow always afraid of losing—no matter how generous you appeared. If you didn't seek wealth or honor, you sought common interest or confidence or understanding.

Take away these comforts and you are pained, hurt, and offended. Doesn't this show who you really love?

When it is God you love in someone, you stand by that person no matter what. If the friendship is broken in the order of God, you are at peace. You may feel a deep pain, for the friendship was a great gift, but it is a calm suffering, and free from the cutting grief of a possessive love. God's love sets you free.

Do not waste your suffering. Let suffering accomplish what God wants it to in your life. Never get so hard that you suffer for no reason and for no purpose. Paul says, "God loves a cheerful giver." How much He must love those who cheerfully give themselves to His dealings.

# Part II

## A Life of Simplicity

# SIMPLE OBEDIENCE

Encourage peace. Become deaf to your over-active imagination. Your spinning imagination will harm your health and make your spiritual life very dry. You worry yourself sick for no good reason. Inner peace, and the sweet presence of God, are chased away by restlessness. How can you hear God speak, in His soft and tender way, when your hurried thoughts create a whirlwind within? Be quiet, and He will soon be heard. Allow yourself one excess: to be excessively obedient.

You ask for comfort, but you do not see that you have been led to the edge of the fountain and refuse to drink. Peace and comfort are to be found only in simple obedience. Be obedient without a lot of talk about how obedient you are. You will soon find rivers of living water flowing within you. If you believe much, you will receive much. If you believe nothing, you will receive nothing, and continue to listen only to the stories your empty imagination tells you.

You dishonor true love by supposing that it is concerned about the insignificant things that continually occupy your attention. Satan is transformed into an angel of light. He assumes the form

of a legalistic love, and an overly-sensitive conscience. You should know by now the troubles he
will lead you into if he convinces you to be a
Pharisee. Reject his advances.

If you allow yourself to have only simple and
uncomplicated desires, you will be more pleasing
to God than if you died the death of a hundred
martyrs. Turn your anxieties to the fact that you
have delayed in offering this sacrifice of simplicity
to God. Can true love hesitate when the Well-
Beloved asks?

# THE DANGER OF SPIRITUAL AMBITION

I am happy to hear you are well, and to see that you are telling me, in a simple way, all that takes place within you. Never hesitate to write to me about anything you think God is asking.

It is not surprising that you are very ambitious to advance in your spiritual life, and to find yourself in the company of those who have a reputation for being spiritual. No matter what it looks like, these things still flatter your self-love. Do not seek to fulfill your ambitions of becoming more spiritual, or to be counted in the company of those people who are honored for their spirituality. Your aim should be to die to all such ambitions by letting yourself be humbled. You must learn to accept obscurity and scornful disregard while you keep your eyes solely on God.

You may hear endless sermons about living a perfect life. You may know what everyone preaches about it and still be farther away from perfection than ever. Your deepest aim should be to turn a deaf ear to self, while listening to God in silence. You should renounce your pride and give yourself over to what pleases God. Say little and do much—without wondering if you have been noticed or not.

God will teach you more than even the most mature Christian could. He will teach you better than all the books in the world could. Why are you so eager to chase after knowledge? Don't you realize that all you need is to be poor in spirit, and to know nothing but Christ and Him crucified? *Knowledge puffs up*, it is only *love that builds up*. (I Corinthians 8:1) Be content with love alone.

What! Do you think that the way to love God comes by getting more knowledge? You have already more than you can use. Practice what you already know rather than looking for more knowledge. You deceive yourself if you think you are growing spiritually because your curiosity has intellectually explored some spiritual idea. Humble yourself, and do not expect to receive from man that which God alone can give.

# THE DEPTHS OF PRIDE

You know what God wants from you—how can you refuse? You sense that your resistance to His call comes entirely from self-love. Will you allow your pride to grow and invent more ingenious excuses only to reject God's mercy? You apply so many moral standards to your wandering thoughts—just learn to ignore them. You confess things that are better to disregard. Yet, the fact that you continually resist the Holy Spirit is of no concern to you. Is this because God does not see fit to give you what you want, the way you want it?

Self-interest and pride cause you to reject the gifts of God because they do not come in a way that suits your taste. How can you pray? What is God speaking to you in the depths of your spirit? He asks for nothing but death, but you desire nothing but life. How can you ask Him to answer a prayer only the way you want it answered?

Does it matter if you receive the gifts of grace the way a beggar receives bread? This would not cause the gifts to be less pure or less precious. Receive with humility the sweet grace that God wants to give you.

# THE MASK OF
# THE SELF-NATURE

Selfishly loving yourself shuts the spirit. You put yourself in a straitjacket when you are enclosed in self. When you come out of that prison, you experience how immense God is, and how He sets His children free.

I rejoice that God has reduced you to weakness. You will not be convinced of or delivered from your self-love by any other means. Self-love finds hidden strength and secret hiding places because of your natural strength and ingenuity for survival. You cannot see your selfishness. Self-ishness feeds on the subtle poison of an apparent generosity in always sacrificing for others. God will force your old nature to cry out loud and come out in the open. See how jealous you really are?

Weakness is very painful, but also very useful. While any self-love remains, you are afraid that it will be discovered. As long as the least bit of self-love remains in the secret parts of your heart, God will hunt it down, and, by some infinitely merciful blow, force your selfishness and jealousy out of hiding. The poison then becomes the cure. Self-love, exposed to the light, sees itself in horror. The flattering lifelong illusions you have held of your-self are forced to die. God lets you see who you really worship: yourself. You cannot help but see yourself. And you can no longer hide your true self from others, either.

So to strip self-love of its mask is the most humiliating punishment that can be inflicted. You see that you are no longer as wise, patient, polite, self-possessed, and courageous in sacrificing yourself for others as you had imagined. You are no longer fed by the belief that you need nothing. You no longer think that your "greatness" and "generosity" deserve a better name than "self-love." Now you see your selfishness like that of a silly child, screaming at the loss of an apple. But you are further tormented because you also weep in rage that you have cried at all!

Nothing can comfort you because your poisonous character has been discovered. You see all your foolish rudeness and condescension. Look at your own frightening reflection. Say with Job, "For the thing which I greatly feared is come upon me, and that which I was afraid of is come unto me." (Job 3:25) Good! What your old nature fears the most is necessary for its destruction.

God doesn't need to attack that which is already dead. It is only the living that must die. What you need is to be convinced of your over-sensitivity. All you have to do is to be quietly willing to see yourself as you are. The minute you do, you will begin to change.

You ask for a cure to get well. You do not need to be cured but killed. Do not look for a remedy; let death come. Be careful, however, that you do not courageously decide to let yourself find no remedy. This can be a remedy in disguise, and even this can give aid and comfort to the self-life. Seek no comfort for self-love, and do not hide your disease. Let everything be simply seen, and then allow yourself to die.

This death is not to be accomplished by any of your own strength. Weakness is the only thing you should possess. All strength is out of place. It only makes the agony longer and harder. If you die from exhaustion, you will die more quickly and less violently.

Dying is necessarily painful. Stimulants are a cruelty to those being tortured. They do not want more strength—they long only for the fatal blow. If it were possible to aid the one being tortured by weakening him and hastening his death, his suffering would be shortened. But he can do nothing. The hand that tied him to his torture rack is the only one that can finish him off.

Do not ask for cures or strength or even death. To ask for death is impatience. To ask for food or remedies is to prolong your agony. What shall you do then? Seek nothing. Hold to nothing. Confess everything, but not to gain comfort, but to gain humility and a desire to yield.

Look to me not as a means of life, but as a means of death. An instrument of life would not serve its purpose if it did not minister life. An instrument of death would be falsely named if it kept people alive rather than killing them. Let me be, or at least seem to be, hard, unfeeling, indifferent, without pity, annoyed, and scornful. God knows how far it is from the truth, but He permits it all to appear this way. I shall be of much more use to you by this false and imaginary character than through my affection and real assistance. The point is not to know how you are to be kept alive, but how you are to lose everything and die.

# WRONG MOTIVATION

There is something deceptively wrong with the way you deal with your suffering. While on the outside you seem to be only concerned with the glory of God, the unconquered self-nature deep within is causing you trouble. I am sure that you want God to be glorified, but you want His glory to be expressed through the testimony that He has made you perfect. Let me tell you that this feeds self-love. It is simply a clever disguise of the self-nature.

If you really want to grow from the discovery of your faults, do not justify nor condemn yourself because of them. Instead, quietly bring them before God. Agree with Him about all things—even those you cannot understand.

Remain at peace, for peace is what God wants for you no matter what is happening. There is, in fact, a peace of conscience which sinners should enjoy as they are repenting. Suffering should be peaceful and tempered with God's comfort. Remember the wonderful word of God that once delighted you—*the Lord was not in noise and confusion, but in the still, small voice.* (I Kings 19:11)

# DEALING WITH
# YOUR FAULTS

Don't worry about your faults. You are likely to seek what God can give to you rather than God Himself.

I was just reading about someone who had read the biography of a godly person. He was so angered at his own comparative imperfection that he entirely gave up the idea of living a life devoted to Christ. Don't be like that! If you look at how flawed you are, you will upset yourself and interrupt the presence of God and His perfect work within you. The embarrassment you feel at seeing your own faults is a greater problem than the original faults.

Francis de Sales said that it is easy to become occupied with love rather than with the Well-Beloved. If God was the only object of your affection you would be entirely concerned with Him alone. When you are busy trying to get a sense of the feeling that He loves you, then you are still preoccupied with yourself. The more peaceful and open your spirit, the nearer you will sense your Lord.

# LIVE IN THE
# PRESENT MOMENT

Live in peace without worrying about the future. Unnecessary worrying and imagining the worst possible scenario will strangle your faith. God alone knows what will happen to you. You really don't even own the present moment, for even this belongs to God. So live according to His will.

Each day there is just enough that God gives you to take care of—nothing more or less is expected of you. Who are you to ask the Lord, "Why are you doing this to me?" He is the Lord—let Him do what seems good to Him. You certainly don't need to add your wisdom and your plans to His wise and good plan. Eating the fruit of your own wisdom is always a bitter experience. God allows this to show you how unpleasant it is to ignore His guidance. The future is not yet yours—perhaps it never will be. And when tomorrow comes it will probably be different from what you had imagined.

It isn't enough to separate yourself from the world's ways. You also must allow humility to be formed within you. Separation from the world means turning away from external things. When humility is formed in you, then you will turn away

46

from your own self-nature.

Every trace of pride must be conquered. Your pride in thinking you know much about spiritual things is more dangerous than being very rich. Pride helps you believe you are something important in a much more subtle way.

Put aside your self-interest, and simply let God's will unfold around you. Everything He does for you is for your good. Worship Him without having to know and see everything. Continue doing the good things that you do, since you feel that you should and can do them so easily. Avoid things which distract you from Christ, and be careful that all your extra energy does not lead you into trouble. Above all, live in the present moment and God will give you all the grace you need.

# DEALING WITH OFFENSES

Of course I sympathize with all your trials. The only thing I can do is pray that God will comfort you. You really need the Spirit of God to give you strength in your trials. His spirit will hold back the overpowering nature of your natural strength. It is natural to want to defend yourself against the problems you now face. But do not fight them with your own strength.

As far as the letter regarding your birth, I think you should give it to God. Ask for God's mercy on the one who wants to hurt you. I have always sensed that you were sensitive about this point.

God always attacks you on your weak side. You do not try to kill someone by hitting him where he is the strongest. You must aim for his vital organs: the seat of his life. When God aims to kill your old self-nature, He touches the tenderest spot—the spot full of life! This is why he gives you the kinds of trials that He does.

Allow yourself to be humbled. If you are silent and peaceful when humiliating things happen to you, you will grow in grace. I realize that you will be tempted to defend yourself for a thousand different reasons. But it is far better to be humbly silent. Humility that can still talk needs to be carefully watched. You will comfort yourself too much when you speak out.

Don't be so upset when things are said about you. Let the world talk; just seek to do the will of God. You will never be able to entirely satisfy people and it isn't worth the painful effort. Silent peace and sweet fellowship with God will repay you for every evil word spoken against you. Love your neighbor without expecting his friendship. People will come and go—let them do as they please. See only God. He is the One that afflicts or comforts you through people and circumstances. He does this for your benefit.

# DISTRACTIONS

I pray that this new year will be a year full of grace and blessing to you. I am not surprised that you do not enjoy inward prayer as you first did. Every pleasure is likely to be exhausted. An active personality, accustomed to lots of activity, will faint in solitude. For a long time you have been distracted by much outward activity. I am aware of the trouble you will encounter as you seek to live a life totally given over to God's will.

At first the sheer strength of your enthusiasm will carry you through your problems, no matter how large. When you feel strong, you feel that you can do anything. When you are discouraged, you think that you can do nothing and that all is lost. But both of these ways are wrong.

Do not be disturbed by any distraction you experience in prayer. The distractions are deep within you, even when you want to pray inwardly. Your temperament and habits all help make you very active. Only when you are completely exhausted will you seek a quieter life.

By being fruitful you will gradually come to experience a deeper inward life with fewer distractions. God gave you a foretaste of it before in order that you might see where He wanted to lead you. He then takes this wonderful taste away so that you can see that it does not belong to you. See clearly that everything He gives is a gift of grace which must be received in humility.

Do not be surprised to find yourself overly sensitive, impatient, proud, and self-willed. Realize that this is your natural disposition. Augustine says you must bear the yoke of the daily confession of your sins. Learn to feel your own weakness, waywardness, and inability to correct yourself. Despair of your own heart and hope only in God. Bear with yourself, but do not flatter yourself into thinking you are better than you are. Do not neglect anything needed for your correction.

See your true character, but wait on God's timing to transform it. Let yourself become lowly under His all-powerful hand. Anytime you sense any resistance in your will, yield yourself to God. Cultivate silence as much as possible. Be in no hurry to judge. Hold back your decisions, your likes and dislikes. Stop at once when your activity becomes too hurried. Do not be eager even for good things.

# LISTEN TO GOD

Don't listen to your self-nature. Self-love whispers in one ear and God whispers in the other. The first is restless, bold, eager, and reckless; the other is simple, peaceful, and speaks but a few words in a mild, gentle voice. As soon as you listen to the loud voice of self you will not hear the soft tones of holy love. Each speaks only of one thing. Self-love speaks only of self—it never gets enough attention. Self-love talks of being well thought of. The self despairs of everything except downright flattery.

God's love, on the other hand, whispers that self should be forgotten—counted as nothing so that God might be all. God wants to completely fill you and unite Himself to you. Let the vain, complaining babble of self-love be silenced so that in the stillness of the heart you may listen to the love of God.

While you live on earth you can understand only in part. The self-love, which is the source of your faults, is also what hides your faults. Self-love must be rooted out of you so that God can reign within you without opposition.

The light of God will show you what you are really like, and will also heal you of your sins.

Until you see yourself in God's pure light, you really don't know yourself. You really rely on yourself much more than you think.

God's love will cause you to see clearly that He loves you without partiality and without flattery. This is how you must see yourself, as well as your neighbor. But relax, God only shows you your weakness as He gives you the courage to bear the sight! You will be shown your imperfections one by one as you are able to face them. Unless God gives you grace to see your weaknesses, the knowledge of them would only lead to despair.

Those who correct others should watch for the Holy Spirit to go ahead of them and touch a person's heart. Learn to imitate Him who reproves gently. People do not need to see God condemning them, they must realize within themselves that they have done something wrong. Do not be heavy-handed lest people see God as a judgmental ogre. When you become outraged over a person's fault, it is generally not "righteous indignation" but your own impatient personality expressing itself. Here is the imperfect pointing a finger at the imperfect. The more you selfishly love yourself, the more critical you will be. Self-love cannot forgive the self-love it discovers in others. Nothing is so offensive to a haughty, conceited heart as the sight of another one.

God's love, however, is full of consideration, patience, and tenderness. It leads people out of their weakness and sin one step at a time. The less selfish you are, the more considerate you will be of others. Wait a long time, wait years, before giving advice. And then only give advice as God opens the hearts of those who are to receive it. If you pick fruit before the fruit ripens, you will spoil it completely.

Your imperfect friends, and we are all imperfect, can only know you imperfectly. They see in you what you cannot see and overlook much that you do see. They are quick to see things that offend them, but they do not look deep within to the faults that are deeply hidden. Even their best judgments are superficial.

Listen to the voice of God in silence. Be willing to accept what He wants to show you. God will show you everything you need to know. Be faithful to come before Him in silence. When you hear the still, small voice within, it is time to be silent. This voice is not a stranger to your spirit. It is God's voice within your spirit. This is not something mystical but something practical. Deep within you will learn to yield to God and to trust your Lord.

# LET GO OF ANXIETY

Let your anxiety flow away like a stream. What evidence you concoct for the most imaginary situations! God permits you, despite your excellent sense, to be blind to what is right in front of you. You think you see clearly what does not exist at all. God will be glorified in your life if you yield to Him. Never make important decisions in a state of distress. You just are not able to see clearly.

When you are calm and collected, you will find the will of God more clearly known. Turn toward devotion and simplicity. Listen to God and be deaf to yourself. When you are in a place of calm and quiet rest, do all that you sense within your spirit. But to suppose you are level-headed when you are in the agony of distress is to set yourself up to make a mistake. Any experienced spiritual counselor will tell you not to make decisions until you regain your peace and re-enter inward prayer. Never trust yourself when you are suffering greatly because your nature is so unreasonable and upset.

You say that I am trying to prevent you from doing what you should. God forbid! I do not want to encourage you or stop you. I only want you to please God. It is as clear as day that you will fail to do what God wants if you act when your old nature is feeling deeply wounded to the point of despair. Would you do something only to make yourself happy even if it went against God's will? God forbid. Wait until you are not feeling so hurt. Be open to every alternative that God might suggest. Sacrifice anything for His sake.

# QUIET LEADING

I know that God will keep you. Although you do not enjoy spiritual discipline, be faithful to seeking God as much as your health will permit. I realize that eating, both physically and spiritually, does not appeal to you now. Still, you must eat to survive.

It would be good for you if you could have a few minutes of fellowship with those members of your family that you can confide in. As to whom you should talk with—be guided by your inner sense of what is right in each moment. God does not lead you with extreme emotion, and for this I am glad. Remain faithful to the still, small voice.

Strong emotions and deep feelings, or seeking after signs, can be more dangerous than helpful. Your imagination is sure to run away with you. God will lead you, almost without your knowing it, if you will be faithful to come before Him quietly. Eat of Him and His word. Love Him and I will tell you to do no more. For if you love Him, everything else will work out. I am not asking you for a tender and emotional love, but simply that you lean toward love. Put God before yourself and the world and even your evil desires will begin to be transformed.

# ACCEPT YOUR WEAKNESS

I hear you are sick. I suffer with you for I dearly love you. Still, I cannot help but kiss the hand that allows this illness. I pray that you will lovingly kiss it with me. You have abused your good health and this is the result.

God will not only show you how physically weak you are, but how spiritually weak you are without Him. How strong you will be when you see that you are completely weak. Then you will always be able to believe that you are mistaken. Open yourself to the insight of others. Do not be dogmatic. Speak the truth simply.

Allow others to evaluate you, but judge no one. Offer advice only to those who ask for it. Mention the faults of others without being heavy-handed or legalistic. And do not speak to gain a good reputation for yourself.

I pray that God will keep you faithful to His grace. "He that has begun a good work in you will perform it until the day of Jesus Christ." (Philippians 1:6) Patiently bear with yourself. Give to the Lord all that annoys you. Do this quietly and peacefully. And do not expect things to change in a single day.

Think little and do much. If you are not

careful, you will acquire so much knowledge that you will need another lifetime to put it all into practice. There is danger in thinking that you are perfect simply because you understand what it would be like to be perfect. All your beautiful theories do not help you die to yourself. Knowledge nourishes the life of Adam in you because you secretly delight in your revelation. Never trust your own power or your own knowledge. Be humble. Do not trust your old nature.

# LET THINGS GO

Your mind is too busy and you are too argumentative to maintain a quiet awareness of God. If
you are always reasoning, then you cannot cultivate the silence in which God speaks. Be humble,
sincere, and simple with people. Be calm and quiet
before God.

Your mentors are too dry and intellectual and
critical. These people oppose an inward spiritual
life. Even if you only listen to them a little, you
will be drawn out of a quiet and simple faith. They
reason too much and they are unhealthily curious.
Long-standing habits are easily restarted, because
you already have a natural leaning toward them.
Stay away from anything that will lead you down
old paths.

It has been four months since I have had any
time to study. But I am glad to give up study and
not cling to anything that God wants to take away.
Perhaps this winter I will have time to set foot in
my library. I shall enter it cautiously and listen for
the slightest hint that God would have me else-
where. The mind must fast as well as the body. I
have no desire to write, speak or be spoken about,
reason, or persuade anybody.

I live each day simply. I put up with any

inconveniences which present themselves, but I also take the time for entertainment when I need to do so. Those who write things against me and are afraid of me are sadly deceived. God bless them! I am not so foolish as to go out of my way to annoy them. As Abraham said to Lot: "Is not the whole land before you? If you go to the east, I will go to the west." (Genesis 13:9)

Happy are the free! Only Jesus can make you free. He sets you free by snapping every chain that holds you. How? His sword divides husband and wife, father and son, brother and sister. As long as anything in this world means anything to you, your freedom is only a word. You are like a bird that is held by a leash; you can only fly so far. You see what I mean? What you stand to gain is more valuable than all that you fear you will lose. Be faithful with what you know and more will be given to you. Do not trust your mind too much— how many times has it led you astray?

My own mind has been such a deceiver that I no longer count on it. Be simple. "The way of this world passes away." (I Corinthians 7:31) You will pass away with the world if you pattern yourself after it. God's truth remains forever, so let His ways fully take hold of you.

I warn you again: Beware of philosophers. They will trap you and do you more harm than you know how to do them good. Their discussions go on forever, yet they never come to the simple truth. Intellectuals are unwisely curious; they are like conquerors who destroy the world without possessing it. Solomon himself testifies to the vanity of endless reasoning.

Never study spiritual subjects unless God prompts you to. And do not study more than you can use. Study with a prayerful spirit. God is both Truth and Love. You can only know the truth to the degree that you love. Love the truth and you will understand the truth. If you do not love, you do not know love. Love with a humble heart and the Truth will love you. You will know what philosophers cannot know and even what philosophers do not want to know. I hope that you will obtain the knowledge that is kept for babes and the simple-minded. Such knowledge is hid from the wise and prudent. (Matthew 6:25)

# AVOID
# SPIRITUAL BUSYBODIES

I am glad that you have found the qualities you were looking for in the person you told me about. God puts what He pleases where He pleases. He sends us help and light through many different people and circumstances. Should this matter to you? If you see that God is sending you the help, then you will not be so taken up with how He sent it. His ways are high above ours.

Trust His way and you will grow in humility and simplicity. The Lord will show you that you have no power in and of yourself. Receive what He gives and depend on His Spirit, who blows where He wills. (John 3:8) You do not need to know the secrets of God—just be obedient to what He shows you to do.

Thinking too much will distract you. If you become trapped in your thoughts, they will blow out your inward spiritual sense like a wind blowing out a candle. If you keep company with people like this, you will see how dry their hearts are and how far their minds have drifted off center. It is best to stay away from such people.

I also want to warn you about people who appear to have an inward spiritual life. It is easy to mistake a vivid imagination for true spiritual experience. Watch carefully and you will see that they are still improperly attached to outward things. Your wayward desires, left unattended, will lead to obsessions that strangle your inner peace and silence before God. Stay away from people who sound good but never exhibit true fruit of an inward walk. Their talk is deceptive and you will almost always find them restless, fault-finding, and full of their own thoughts.

These spiritual busybodies are annoyed with everything, and are almost always annoying!

# BE SATISFIED
# WITH TODAY

I pray that you never look for what you can get by trusting God, nor even cling to the things of this life, no matter how important they seem to you. Trust completely in God. He will not deceive you, but trusting the dark desires still hidden in your heart will.

Be as lowly and simple among the prestigious as you are alone before God. Do nothing from your natural reasoning. Look for no sense of certainty. Do not even look forward to better things. The present moment is your sole treasure for here is where the will of God is found. Do not insult today by looking for a better tomorrow! You deserve to be disappointed when you seek comfort like that!

Receive everything with a lowly spirit. Watch out that your curiosity does not cause you to seek things you shouldn't. Watch out, too, for selfishness that would want to hold back something good. Let God work, and view each moment as if it were the whole sweep of eternity.

# TURN YOUR BACK
# ON YOURSELF

Your only task is to bear the weaknesses of your body and mind. Strength is made perfect in weakness. You are only strong in God when you are weak in yourself. Your weakness will be your strength if you accept it with a lowly heart.

You will be tempted to believe that weakness and lowliness are not part of trusting God. It is commonly believed that to trust God you generously give God everything because you love Him so much. Heroic sacrifices are held up as true examples of trusting God. To truly trust God is not so glamorous.

Trusting in God is a simple resting in God's love, as a baby lies in its mother's arms. Perfect trust means you must turn your back on yourself without even being aware that you have turned your back. Sounds impossible, doesn't it? But I tell you that there is no deeper trust of yourself than knowing that you trust God completely.

The point of trusting God is not to do great things that you can feel good about, but to trust God from a place of deep weakness. Here is a way to know if you've actually trusted God with something—you will not think about the matter any longer, nor will you feel a lack of peace.

# OPEN YOUR HEART

You sense within you what God wants, yet you resist. No wonder you are distressed. You say, "It is impossible to do what God wants." Now that is a real invitation to despair, isn't it? Despair of yourself as much as you like, but never despair of God. You know that He is all-good and all-powerful. God will give to you according to your faith. Look at Abraham who hoped against hope! Look at Mary who did not hesitate even when the most incredible thing in the world was proposed to her!

Open your heart. You have shut it so tightly you do not even want God to help you at this point. How can grace find room to work with an attitude like that? All I ask is that you rest in faith with a teachable spirit. Do not listen to yourself. Give in to the will of God with a humble heart. God will work everything out for you. The things that look the largest and most impossible will be accomplished without your even knowing how.

By the circumcision of your heart you are made children of Abraham. Like him you must leave your native country and all that is familiar to you, and go out without even knowing where you are going. What a blessing! Leave everything and deliver yourself up to a God who loves you jealously! You, by yourself, can only accomplish shallow changes. You do not know yourself. God knows you deeply, and knows exactly where to dig up the source of your troubles. Self-love is cowardly. The self does not have the courage to wound itself to death. The hand of God strikes in unexpected places and leaves nothing uncovered. Your self-love will cry out where God hits it. See to it that you do nothing to comfort it. Just sit back and let God do His work. Stay still as He operates on you and His work will be a success.

I am inspired by John the Baptist who completely forgot himself that he might think only of Christ. He pointed to Christ with his whole life. What an example he sets before you!

# LIVE OUT GOD'S TRUTH

As you read a passage from the Scriptures, pause after each verse or phrase to hear what God might be saying. Consider how Jesus practices what you are reading. Think how other faithful believers live out God's truth. Consider what may keep you from living the truth out yourself. As you sense your inability to live out some truth, come before God humbly and silently. See clearly how incapable you are. Ask God to live His life in you, and to do for you all that you cannot do yourself. He will certainly finish the work that He started in you.

Let me give you an example. Suppose you are reading John 17. In this passage Jesus says to His Father: "I have glorified You on earth; I have finished the work which You gave me to do." Everyone has his own work but not everyone is doing the work which God has given him to do. Everything that you do from pride, or to move up in the eyes of the world, or merely because it pleases your old nature is not the work that God gives you. All this kind of work is from the world, or the flesh, or even the devil.

What God wants you to do is work on those things that are out of line with His nature within you. He wants to replace your old nature with His very own nature. This will mean new thoughts and desires. Here is the work of God. Consider the example of the believers that have gone before you. Some of them had a much harder time than you do. They were weak, too, but they finished their spiritual race.

You are not speaking on God's behalf when you exhibit a temper that is out of control. His work begins in you by your wanting to turn away from your old life. Gentleness is Your work, my God. Here is the work that You have given me to do.

Perhaps God has called you to endure being poorly served. Do so gladly, for it will certainly please God. Remember that you are not called to be well-served, but to serve Him well. Learn to be gentle and patient with all that disturbs you.

Each day is full of many such matters and you will learn to deal with them. Each of these events will teach you to live in the presence of God. Do not trust your good intentions if they do not produce a sense of life within you. Seek to become gentle and humble. If you do something wrong that only affects you, then quietly repent of it. If you have wronged others, perhaps with a nasty word, then do them some little act of kindness. Remember how gently and patiently God deals with you. Watch Him deal with you and from that learn to deal with others. Do not be discouraged by your mistakes. Continually come back to God.

# CULTIVATING SILENCE

Simply bringing yourself quietly before God will do more than worrying or being too religious. Silence is so important. Even when you cannot find total silence, you might try letting others take the lead in conversations. There is no better way to quench the natural strength of your old nature than by silencing it. Guard your tongue. As you become more aware of the presence of God within, you will see how He is able to keep your words, thoughts, and desires in check. This work all happens gradually, so be patient with yourself as well as with others.

Try to practice silence as much as general courtesy permits. Silence encourages God's presence, prevents harsh words, and causes you to be less likely to say something you will regret. Silence also helps you put space between you and the world. Out of the silence that you cultivate, you will find strength to meet your needs.

No matter how much you cultivate silence, there will still be many disrupting situations in which you will find yourself against your will. God knows that you want to have much time to pray, but He still allows you to be surrounded by things that seem to prevent prayer.

Learn to love God's will more than the sweetness of self-chosen prayer. You know very well that you do not need to pray in your closet to love God. When He gives you time, take it to pray. When there is not time, be satisfied anyway. Lift up your spirit to Him without making any outward sign. Talk only when necessary. Bear the hardest things that cross your life. You need to deny yourself more than you need more light. Be faithful in keeping silent, and God will keep you from evil when you talk.

Accept what God chooses for you. This is more important than what you choose for yourself, for you are much too easy on yourself. Day by day give yourself to God. He carries you in His arms like a mother carries her child. Believe, hope, and love like a child. Look with love and trust to your heavenly Father.

# LIVE
# MOMENT BY MOMENT

It is a great gift to be able to be peaceful when you are facing situations that do not seem to change. Bear all the uncomfortable and inconvenient things about your current situation. Look at them as exercises that God has designed for your growth. He is teaching you to bear difficult situations without being depressed. Your emotions may be low, but your inner man is being upheld. This peace is all the more precious when there is no earthly reason to have it.

It is wonderful to be willing to accept all situations, no matter how difficult. It is good to never say, "This is all too much for me, I cannot bear it." Depend on the Almighty. God's hand holds you. Do not try to look too far ahead, but merely live moment by moment before God. Yield to God with a heart full of trust. The more God loves you, the less He spares you. Accept what comfort He gives you. Live to do His will alone.

# WORK OUT YOUR SALVATION

Be faithful to God in small things. Most people spend most of their life regretting their bad habits. They talk about turning over a new leaf, but they never actually get down to working out their own salvation. In every moment you have the privilege to enter more fully into your salvation. As God gives you each moment, use it. You have no guarantee about tomorrow.

Listen to God, live in His presence, and avoid things that draw you away from Him. Find Him within you, and pour out your heart to Him. Love Him above everything. Submit your plans to His will. Find out what He wants for you and then do it quickly. Small things become great when they are done as God wills.

Do not try to make judgments about how important something is if God asks it of you. Do what God asks you out of love and obedience to Him—this is enough.

No matter how difficult or uncomfortable your circumstances become, you are free because you have come to accept them all from the hand of God. The greatest thing is to suffer without being discouraged.

# TURN TOWARD GOD

You need to take time to turn to God. Do not pray only when you have set aside time to do so. The busier you are, the more you must practice turning to God. If you wait until the time is convenient, there is little doubt that you will end up spending little time with God.

Try to come before God both in the morning and the evening. Pray during and between all your other jobs as much as you can. You cannot retire too much from the mindless chatter of the world. Learn to steal this time in little snatches, and you will find these moments the most precious part of your day.

You don't need much time to tell God that you love Him! Lift your heart to Him. Worship Him in the depths of your spirit. Offer Him what you do and what you suffer. Tell God the most important things that occur to you; tell Him what stands out to you as you read the Bible. Cling to your dearest Friend; live in Him with unbounded trust; speak to Him out of a heart full of love. As you learn to continually turn your spirit toward the loving presence of God within you, you will find yourself strengthened to do what is required of you. Here is the kingdom of God coming to life within.

These times of inward retirement are the only solution for your quick temper, critical nature, and impatience. Turning to God will help you, but you will need to do it frequently.

As God draws you to Himself, follow Him with complete trust. Love Him as you would wish to be loved. Does this sound extravagant? It is not giving Him too much. As He shows you new ways to love Him, then do so.

Speak and act without too much planning and self-examination. Set your eyes on God and you will feel less of a need to please others. The wonderful thing is that you may end up pleasing them more.

# LEAN TOWARD HIM

Try, without forcing yourself, to turn to God and touch Him as often as you can. Even when you want to touch the Lord and you are distracted, it is important to keep bringing yourself before Him. Do not wait for a perfectly quiet time when you can lock yourself in your room and be alone. You know how hard it is to find such a time. The very moment you feel drawn toward God is the moment to turn toward Him. Simply lean toward Him with a heart full of love and trust. Do this when you are driving or dressing or getting your hair done. Turn toward Him while you are eating or others are talking. When conversation becomes boring, during a business meeting, for instance, you can find a few moments to fellowship with your Father instead of being drained by unnecessary talk.

Be faithful to your times of prayer whether or not you find any comfort in them. Make use of the time during the day when you are only slightly busy. Occupy every spare second with God. Even when you are doing needlework you can be aware of God's presence. It is harder to be aware of His presence when you are engaged in a conversation, but you can learn to sense Him within you, monitoring your words, and restraining all outbreaks of pride, hatred, and self-love. Do your work steadily and reliably. Be patient with yourself.

Something else you should remember is to watch your actions and hold yourself back if you see yourself about to do something wrong. If you do something wrong, bear the humiliation of your error. But try to yield immediately to the warning the Holy Spirit is giving you within. Faults done in haste or because of human weakness are nothing compared to closing your ear to the inner voice of the Holy Spirit.

And if you do commit a sin, realize that getting upset and feeling sorry for yourself will do no good. Pick yourself up and go on without letting your pride get its feathers ruffled.

Admit you were wrong, ask forgiveness, then go on. Being irritated with yourself is not what it means to pick yourself up and go on in peace. Don't be so upset by your mistakes.

Often what you offer God is not what He wants. He usually wants that which you dread giving Him. It is Isaac, the well-beloved, that He wants you to give up. What He is after is what comes between you and Him. He will not rest, and neither will you, I might add, until you have given Him everything. If you want to prosper and enjoy God's blessing, don't hold anything back from Him. What comfort, freedom, and strength there is when nothing stands between you and God.

# COME OUT OF YOURSELF

As long as you live by your old nature you will be open to all of the injustices of men. Your temper will get you into fights, your passions will clash with your neighbors, your desires will be like tender spots open to your enemies' arrows. Everything will be against you–attacking you from all sides. If you live at the mercy of a crowd of greedy and hungry desires, then you will never find peace. You will never be satisfied because everything will bother you. You will be like an invalid who has been bedridden for many years–anywhere you are touched you will feel pain. Your self-love is terribly touchy. No matter how slightly it is insulted, it screams, "Murderer." Add to this all the insensitivity of others, their disgust at your weakness (and your disgust at theirs), and you have the children of Adam forever tormenting each other.

The only hope is to come out of yourself. Lose all your self-interest. Only then can you enjoy the true peace reserved for "men of good will." Such people have no other will but God's. If you come to such a place, then what can harm you? You will no longer be attacked through your hopes or fears. You may be worried, inconvenienced, or distressed, but you can rest in Him. Love the hand that disciplines you. Find peace in all things— even in going to the cross. Be happy with what you have. Wish for nothing more. Surrender to God and find true peace.

# LIVE DAY BY DAY

Your spiritual walk is a little too restless and uneasy. Simply trust God. If you come to Him, He will give you all that you need to serve Him. You really need to believe that God keeps His word. The more you trust Him, the more He will be able to give you. If you were lost in an uncrossable desert, bread would fall from heaven for you alone.

Fear nothing but to fail God. And do not even fear that so much that you let it upset you. Learn to live with your failures, and bear with the failures of your neighbors. Do you know what would be best for you? Stop trying to appear so mentally and spiritually perfect to God and man. There is a lot of refined selfishness and complacency in not allowing your faults to be revealed. Be simple with God. He loves to communicate Himself to simple people. Live day by day, not in your own strength, but by completely surrendering to God.

# HOPE AND FEAR

Nothing is as difficult to deal with as the tension between hope and fear. Being too sensitive tempts you to believe that your trials are greater than your strength. You do not know the strength of your own heart, nor how much God will try you. God sees everything—the secret depths of your heart and how deeply He must deal with you. Learn to leave these proportions to Him. What you believe is impossible may be only softness and cowardice. What you think is overwhelming may really only overwhelm your pride and self-love—which cannot be crushed too much.

Do not be afraid to sit silently in God's presence. But do not think that this makes you spiritually mature. You cannot use God's presence to escape dealing with your weaknesses. And do not let your devotions neglect your necessary duties. Be sincere, humble, and cooperative with those who have authority.

Open your heart to God's love and receive His strength. As long as you set your whole heart and spirit upon Him, cling to His will, and do not neglect what is required of you, you will not be deceived. Follow God.

# PATIENCE

Anything that resembles pride or a spirit of ridicule reveals a person that is full of himself. This sort of person doesn't see his own faults but takes pleasure in the hard times of others. Here is your self-nature at its worst: easily wounded, full of contempt, haughty, jealous, unforgiving, and lacking graciousness.

You and I are not perfect. You must be patient with your faults and with the faults of others. Be practical about your expectations. No one will become perfect in a day. Even the most perfect people have many imperfections—this means that you have many faults, too! If you are impatient with the faults of others it only shows you how imperfect you are. Your faults and my faults make getting along with one another a hard thing! But we can only fulfill the law of Christ by bearing with each other.

On the other hand, do not excuse your faults or the faults of others. Let your love, patience, and willingness to overlook shortcomings flow between you and all you associate with. Do not pick at other's faults. No one enjoys that and it only pushes people farther away from what is right. You may even cause someone to become so discouraged that they turn back after making their first wobbly steps toward God. Give up your critical nature and stay in touch with Christ within you. Encourage yourself and those around you to give up pride and selfishness.

Live a simple life before God. Accept what God allows in your life. His mercy is what has allowed these events to take place.

Do not let yourself get inwardly irritated by the small troubles and problems that cross your life. Endure them as you would a headache without making them worse than they are. Meanwhile, go about your inward prayer as usual. When things are difficult in your life, prayer will be harder, love will be less tender, and God's presence will be less easily felt. Just learn to be faithful during these trying times—that is all that God asks. It is greater strength that carries a boat against the wind for a quarter of a knot, than for an entire knot with the wind helping you. Treat the complaints of your self-nature as some people treat their spoiled appetites. Do not listen to them and act as if you did not feel them.

# DEPEND ON GOD

The best place to be is where God puts you. Any other place is undesirable because you chose it for yourself. Do not think too much about the future. Worrying about things that haven't happened yet is unhealthy for you. God Himself will help you, day by day. There is no need to store things up for the future. Don't you believe that God will take care of you?

A life of faith does two things: Faith helps you see God behind everything that He uses. And faith also keeps you in a place where you are not sure what will happen next. To have faith you cannot always want to know what is happening or going to happen. God wants you to trust Him alone from minute to minute. The strength He gives you in one minute is not intended to carry you through the next. Let God take care of His business. Just be faithful to what God asks of you. To depend on God from moment to moment—especially when all is dark and uncertain—is a true dying to your old self. This process is so slow and inward that it is often hidden from you as well as others.

When God takes something away from you, you can be sure He knows how to replace it. There is a story that when Paul was alone in the desert, a raven brought him half a loaf of bread every day. If Paul's faith wavered and he wanted to be sure to have enough, he might have prayed that the raven would bring enough for two days. Do you think the raven would have come back at all? Eat in peace what God gives you. "Tomorrow will take care of itself." (Matthew 6:34) The One who feeds you today will surely feed you tomorrow.

# INNER CALM

I hear you are having problems sleeping. You must wait for sleep in peace. If you let your imagination run away with you when you are trying to sleep, you may never get to sleep. I will not think that you are growing spiritually until I see that you have become calm enough to sleep peacefully without restlessness.

Ask God for calmness and inner rest. I know what you are thinking—that controlling your imagination does not depend on yourself. Excuse me, please, but it depends very much on yourself! When you cut off all the restless and unprofitable thoughts that you can control, you will greatly reduce all those thoughts which are involuntary. God will guard your imagination if you do your part in not encouraging your wayward thoughts.

Live in peace. Your imagination is too active; it will eat you up! Your inward life will die of starvation. All that buzzing in your mind is like bees in a beehive. If you excite your thoughts, they will grow angry and sting you! How can you expect God to speak in His gentle and inward voice when you make so much noise? Be quiet and you will hear God speak. Live in the peace of Jesus.

# MISUNDERSTANDING PRAYER

Return to prayer and inward fellowship with God no matter what the cost. You have withered your spirit by chasing this wish of yours without knowing if God wanted this for you.

Don't spend your time making plans that are just cobwebs—a breath of wind will come and blow them away. You have withdrawn from God and now you find that God has withdrawn the sense of His presence from you. Return to Him and give Him everything without reservation. There will be no peace for you otherwise. Let go of all your plans—God will do what He sees best for you.

Even if you were able to accomplish your plans through earthly means, God would not bless them. Offer Him your tangled mess and He will turn everything toward His own merciful purpose. You must learn to let go of everything whether God ever gives you what you so eagerly desire or not. The most important thing is to go back to communion with God—even if it seems dry and you are easily distracted.

# DON'T ESCAPE

I am afraid that you will throw yourself too deeply into your daily activities to escape the painful circumstances you find yourself in. You need to come to God and renew His presence within you during the day.

Live in God's peace. Do what is expected of you while inwardly looking to the Lord. He alone is worthy of your love.

Whenever you become aware of your old nature prompting you to do something, immediately turn away from its suggestion. God's grace will then be able to keep you from falling into sin.

Don't help your old nature out at all. Learn to sabotage every plan your self-nature presents to you. Turn away from every evil alliance. When you are faithful in this way, it is almost as good for your body as it is for your spirit and soul. Do not neglect your duties, but do not be consumed with them.

# SELF-KNOWLEDGE

While you wait for God to deliver you from yourself, you need to take a good look at what you are like. Do not be surprised when you see yourself as you really are—impatient, stubborn, quick-tempered, and arrogant. You must learn to be patient with yourself without cutting yourself any slack. Humble yourself beneath His hand.

Yield to God the first minute you feel yourself resisting. Dwell in silence as much as you can. Avoid choosing your own way, and withhold your opinion as much as possible. Rein yourself in when you see yourself getting too eager. Even if something appears good to you, do not follow it too quickly.

What I want for you is the calmness of heart that comes from sitting before God with a heart full of love for Him. Don't become preoccupied with outward matters. Take care of your affairs in due season with a calm, quiet attention. You will accomplish more by quietly working in the presence of God than by the restless activity that comes from your old nature.

# STEADINESS

Do not let your faults discourage you. Be patient with yourself as well as with your neighbor. Thinking too much will exhaust you and cause you to make a lot of mistakes. Learn to pray in all your daily situations. Speak, act, and walk as if you were in prayer. This is how you should live anyway.

Do everything without becoming too excited. As soon as you start to feel yourself getting too eager, quiet yourself before God. Listen to Him as He prompts you inwardly, then do only as He directs. If you do this, your words will be fewer but more effective. You will be calm, and good will be accomplished in greater measure.

I am not talking about continually trying to reason things out. Simply ask your Lord what He wants of you. This simple and short asking is better than your long-winded inner debates.

Turn toward God and it will be much easier to turn away from your strong natural feelings. Depend on the Lord within you. Your life will eventually become a prayer. You may suffer, but it will be in peace.

# LETTING GO

You must let go of your restlessness, your excessive curiosity, your longing for success, and your habit of collecting things that stroke your ego.

The best way to let go of these things is to cultivate an inner silence where you may come to experience your Lord's presence. If you do this every day of your life, you will make real progress in denying yourself.

Sitting in your Lord's presence will calm you, soften your temper, humble your know-it-all attitude, and restrain your impatience. You will be made aware of your Lord, and the needs of your neighbor. God has blessed you in making you so sensitive. Things that would hardly bother other people touch you to the core. You are troubled or pleased by nothing halfway! But I warn you to guard yourself against your likes and dislikes since they are so passionately expressed.

# INNER REALITIES

Avoid anything that drains or excites you. Your prayer life will dry up if you don't. Don't expect to feed your inward life if you live only for what is outward. You really must learn to renounce all that makes you too outspoken in your conversation. How are you going to cultivate an inner silence if you are always talking? You cannot want God and the things of the world at the same time. Don't you realize that your prayer will be affected by what you cultivate in your daily life?

Fear your excessive enthusiasm, your taste for things of the world, and your hidden ambitions. Don't get so excited over politics and parties. If you get too worked up, it will be harder to calm yourself before God. Speak little and work steadily. Let actions take the place of your flowery words.

After you learn to deal with your wandering thoughts, you must learn to come to God to renew your strength. Learn to do this even amidst the mundane tasks of the day. Keep looking to the Lord for His gentle leading. But don't be so noisy that you can't hear Him!

You will lose your way the minute you decide

to go your own way. When you seek God's will alone, you find it everywhere, and you cannot go astray. Wanting what God wants always puts you on a straight path.The future is not yet yours; it may never be. Live in the present moment. Tomorrow's grace is not given to you today. The present moment is the only place where you can touch the eternal realm.

# STOP STRIVING

You are good, but you want to be better. I think you are trying too hard to use your inner life to change those outward things about you that are socially unacceptable. Deep down you are not really changing. Let me tell you what happens when you don't let God deal with the deepest root of your old nature. You will become very critical, hard-hearted, and pharisaical. You will keep your actions in line according to some self-appointed rules, but deep within you will be unchanged. Outwardly you will appear to obey—but inwardly you will be in a state of rebellion. This is no place to be!

Pay more attention to your inward life. Take your deepest and strongest desires and put them in God's hands. Ask Him to conquer you completely. Give Him your natural arrogance, your worldly wisdom, your attachment to your house, and your fear that no one will recognize your "greatness." You also need to let God deal with your harsh attitude in dealing with things that don't go as you expect them to.

Your temper is not your biggest problem because you already distrust it. In spite of your attempt to control your temper, it still gets the better of you. This humiliation does you good. So worry about your more dangerous faults. I would really rather see you obviously impatient, and lacking a certain amount of self-control. This is more humiliating for you (and better for killing your pride!). When you are too perfect at controlling yourself you can become harsh, judgmental, and too easily offended by others.

Through your weakness learn compassion toward the faults of others. Sincere prayer will soften your heart and make you gentle, kind, and pliable in God's hands. Do you want God to be as critical of you as you are of others?

It is so easy to cling to your "good reputation." Look carefully within yourself. There is somewhere within you a limit which you will not go beyond in offering yourself to Him. You dance around your reservations and make believe that you do not see them. If you let yourself see all your reservations, then you will have to do something about them!

If God ever breaks through your defenses, you will be cut to the quick and left to find all sorts of excuses to justify yourself. The more you hide from giving something up, the more obvious it becomes that you should give it up. If you were truly free you would not spend so much time arguing about it!

Don't bargain with God to get out of this mess in the easiest, most comfortable way. Embrace the cross. Live by love alone. Let God do what He needs to do to root out your self-love. Pray within yourself all day long. Live in prayer—let it touch everything that you do. Be aware of God's presence with you—even when you are busy. Do this and peace will be yours.

You will not become perfect by hearing or reading about perfection. The important thing is not to listen to yourself, but silently listen to God. Talk little and do much, without caring to be seen. God will teach you more than any book or person can. Do you need to go to school to learn how to love God and deny yourself? You already know much more about good than you currently practice. What you need is to put into practice what you already know. Don't try to gain more knowledge before you practice what you already see.

# AVOID LEGALISM

Combine a great amount of exactness with your great freedom. Learn not to exaggerate anything. Speak the truth without embellishment, but do not be hard with it. If you lean too much toward being exact, you will become legalistic. If you try to be free without holding high standards for yourself, you will soon become lazy and careless.

To be truly faithful you must totally obey God. Follow the light which points out the way you should go. Intend to please God in all things. Don't just try to get by with the least amount of obedience. Do the most you can do to please God. I want to tell you, however, not to get caught up trying to figure out if you have committed a "big" sin or a "little" sin. Give everything to God and you will have no need to evaluate your every action.

Don't be depressed when you fail. Just pick yourself up and start all over again. God has a lot of patience with you—learn to have patience with yourself. God will perfect you in His own time. There is no use in always looking over your shoulder to see what has gone wrong. Press on to what is ahead with humility. God is not a spy looking to surprise you. He is not an enemy lurking in the shadows to hurt you. God is your Father who loves you, and wants to help you if you will but trust in His goodness.

It is far better to depend on God to help you because you really cannot help yourself, and neither can you help anyone else on this earth. Trust God and find the path of true freedom.

So I once again say that exactness and freedom go hand in hand. With you I would think that your freedom is outweighed by your strictness. But on the other hand, you are not as strict and committed to total obedience in all areas as I could hope. Learn to trust God and open yourself completely to Him. Completely yield to God as He draws you to Himself.

Do not be afraid to lose sight of yourself and see Him alone. How happy you would be if you were to completely plunge into that ocean of Love. Accept, with a humble heart, all the grace that God pours out to you. This will prepare you, as Teresa of Avila says, for new and fresh gifts from God.

# LOVED ONES

You will never take care of your loved ones so well as when you are faithfully holding them up to God. You, as wise as you may seem, will only get in the way. Only that which comes from God can solve your difficult problems. You, of yourself, cannot convince anyone to turn to God. Life is full of trouble and hard times—God alone holds our hearts in His hand. He strengthens you as He strengthens all who trust in Him. Stay continually in God's presence if you want to lead your flock safely. "Except the Lord keep the city, the watchman watches it in vain." (Psalm 127:1)

You will only hear God speak as you quiet yourself to listen to Him. Does this seem like a waste of time? You will accomplish more in your outward duties by completely leaning on your Lord within. If you want to do the will of your heavenly Father, you will be inwardly fed by discovering that will from God Himself.

# FAULT-FINDING

It seems that you need a larger heart when dealing with others' shortcomings. Why are you so impatient if people don't correct their faults immediately? Everyone has faults. I know that you cannot help seeing them, nor can you prevent yourself from forming opinions about the motives of those who surround you. If you were perfect, you could deal with the imperfections of others without letting them bother you.

Don't be surprised at the defects in good people. God leaves weakness in all of us. In those who are advanced, the weakness is out of proportion to their otherwise mature life. In a field, a workman may leave a pillar of earth to measure the amount of material removed. God leaves similar pillars within those that He is perfecting.

A person with visible shortcomings can be more spiritually advanced than someone who is free from such defects. "Perfect" people often want to find fault with others for not being perfect. Fault-finding, even within yourself, is just soulish enthusiasm. God's way is entirely different. He sometimes allows people to remain deeply flawed in order to keep them from being too satisfied with themselves. It would be easier for them to be corrected of their failings than to feel conquered by their weakness.

People must learn to bear with their own weaknesses as well as the weaknesses of others. Why are you so upset by your neighbors' faults when your own are still uncorrected? Your motives are not entirely pure in wanting to see people perfected for God's glory: People's faults bother you because you are too fussy and hard to please.

You can often help others more by correcting your own faults than theirs. Remember—and you should, because of your own experience—that allowing God to correct your faults is not easy. Be patient with people—wait for God to work with them as He wills.

You need to be more tender-hearted and compassionate toward the faults of others. Let everything that bothers you flow like water under a bridge. Live in the presence of God.

# YIELD YOUR WILL

Love does not depend on your feeling. Your will is what God wants from you. Run your household in a godly way, raise your children properly, and give up empty pleasures. Seek to be simple, quiet, and humble. Let your life be hid with Christ in God. This is what God is after.

When God asks you for something, do not refuse Him. Learn to wait for God. Do not move until He directs you. Each day will bring its own problems. As you deal with them you will grow deeper and deeper in God.

Let your faith strengthen you. When you feel absolutely weak you will discover a strength that is not your own. You will know that the strength is not your own. And if you go astray for a little while, then you will learn humility as you return. Your Lord lives in the center of your spirit. Return to Him there as much as you can. Surrender yourself to God and learn to live by Him rather than out of your own strength. Little by little this learning to live by your Lord's strength unfolds within you. No longer will you cling to things that you can see, but you will cling to God, within you, and there you will find deep and true fellowship.

# COMPLIMENTS

Don't let the compliments you receive from worthy people go to your head. On the other hand, do not let a false humility keep you from accepting God's comfort when He sends it through others.

God wants you to take what comes and not run after what doesn't come. Simply accept what is given to you. Look only to God. Learn to live without those things that God sees fit to take away from you. There are certain things that God wants you to be detached from. Do you see that God allows people to respond to you in many different ways in order to mold you?

Trust God without fear. Learn to accept your weakness as you allow God to change you. There is no use in being impatient or depressed about your faults. Make a habit of inwardly bringing yourself before God as often as you can during the day. Doing this will calm you down.

# SELF-LOVE

You are too self-conscious. You also let your feelings guide you too much. As soon as prayer stops bringing you deep comfort, you become discouraged. Do you want to find peace? Be less infatuated with yourself, and more concerned with pleasing God.

Self-love will let you become sentimental about yourself and overly concerned with your problems. You will find yourself spending all your time worrying about your troubles. Soon all this worry will cloud over the sense of God's presence in your life, and then you will really be depressed. Paul said, "I do not judge myself." Take his advice and you will do well. Give God a free reign to work within you, and then don't spend all your time being introspective.

God will show you what displeases Him and all you have to do is simply turn away from what is unworthy of your Beloved. Stop being so taken up with yourself!

Your old nature wants to be perfect. It will push you in every way to be an outstanding Christian. Please avoid this trap. Simply follow the Lord. You do not need to see yourself as a wise, strong, and virtuous woman. Just be a little child.

# A GOOD EXAMPLE

Teaching is not effective without an example. Begin with acting right, then you can speak later. Be patient. By this I am not saying to indulge people's sins, but rather to not be annoyed when someone makes slow progress. You can easily discourage others by being impatient with them.

The more forceful you are, the more you need to learn gentleness and kindness. Try to understand the needs of the people you care for and adapt yourself to their needs. Show them your heart is open to them and let them know, through experience, that it is safe for them to open their hearts to you without fear. Never be harsh. Be kind and considerate. Decide slowly, but firmly. Correct yourself before you correct others.

# DAILY LIFE

Do one thing: Follow your innermost instinct toward what is good. It was natural for you to follow evil before. Now turn toward following good.

What are you risking to serve God? Your life since your conversion will go on largely as it did before. You will have the same job, and the same daily troubles. But you will have the added comfort of loving the One who is altogether worthy of your love. Your work and suffering for Him will not go unnoticed by Him. He will reward you a hundred times over, even in this life, by the peace that fills your heart. Not only that, but you will live with Him eternally!

No matter what you have to endure as a Christian, you never need lose that deep inward peace. Can the world give you this much? You know as well as I that even people who have everything are still not satisfied.

What are you afraid of? All that you own will eventually leave you. Your possessions cannot fill your spirit. Aren't you tired of the emptiness of your possessions? Don't they secretly tell you that they are not enough? In short, you know your possessions are worthless even as they dazzle you!

What do you fear? Finding a God too good to love? Do you think He will so enamor you that you will not want earthly possessions and the things of this world? Are you afraid to become too humble, too pure, and too grateful to your heavenly Father? Fear nothing but this unfounded fear! It is the world's wisdom that hesitates between you and God, between right and wrong, between thankfulness and ingratitude, between life and death!

Do you really think that God cannot completely satisfy you? Distrust yourself and the opinions of everyone else. You were made to love God and be loved by Him. Never distrust Him. He is the only good One. In His mercy He fills you with dissatisfaction for everything so that you will turn to Him alone.

# RESERVATIONS

I am not surprised that you are disgusted by all that displeases God in your life. This feeling is the natural outcome of your changed heart. You would like a quiet life that lets you attend to your new interests while avoiding the old. This is not the will of God. He wants to let what used to interest you become tiresome, so let this happen as a sort of payment for your past offenses. God will take you out of your old situation when He sees fit. He will do it in His own time.

Meanwhile, come before God regularly. Remember that you carry the gift of God in an earthen pot! Strengthen your inner life through reading, praying, and distrusting your old way of life.

Although you have lived far from Him, you need not be afraid to come to Him like a child. Tell Him how weak and miserable you are, tell Him what you need and what bothers you. You may even tell Him that sometimes you are not exactly thrilled to serve Him. You cannot speak too freely or too truthfully to Him. He likes simple people and talks with them often. Put away all your grand ideas and just be honest with Him. Listen to what He tells you with an open heart. Turn a deaf ear to the world and to your unruly passions.

You will find some help in the books you have read. What you have read is true and will help you lay a good foundation for your faith. Just do not put too much trust in books, and learn to put them aside as God directs. Your mind is a good thing, but learn to distrust it and you will make better use of it. Become childlike. Do even the easiest thing with your heart turned toward God.

Learn to be a good friend. Be willing to help. And by all means maintain a balance in everything you do. There is a certain natural balance that should mark your life as a Christian. Harshness, worry, and severity should not be your trademarks. Rather, learn to live by love. Your Lord within you will direct your actions with ease and simplicity. He will also warn you of approaching danger.

Of course you will suffer problems, illness, and disappointment as other people do, but your attitude toward and reason for bearing these difficulties will be very different from those who do not know God. You can see God in all things, but never so clearly as when you suffer.

Live as you have been and make changes only to avoid what is wrong. Hold true to what is right so that no one will drag you back into sin. You will have an easier time of it when people know that you cannot be swayed from your commitment to God. If you leave yourself open to go astray, you probably will.

Don't trust your own strength, but trust in your Lord who loved you from eternity, before you loved Him.

# CONSISTENCY

I've noticed that you always want to drop one thing to hurry on to the next. Yet each task takes you far too much time to finish because you dissect everything far too much. You are not slow—just long-winded. You want to say everything that has the slightest connection to the subject at hand. This always takes too long and causes you to rush from one thing to another.

Try to be brief. Learn to get to the heart of the matter and disregard the nonessential. Don't spend all your time musing! What you really need to do is sit quietly before God and your active and argumentative mind would soon be calmed. God can teach you to look at each matter with a simple, clear view. You could say what you mean in two words! And as you think and speak less you will be less excitable and distracted. Otherwise you will wear yourself out, and external things will overpower your inward life as well as your health.

Cut all this activity short! Silence yourself inwardly. Come back to your Lord often. You will get more accomplished this way. It is more important to listen to God than to your own thoughts.

It is not enough to like good books. You must be a good book yourself. The people who knew

111

God best had more problems than you, yet they kept their peace and cultivated simplicity, purity, and inward prayer.

I believe that your busy life exhausts you in every way. Don't let your work carry you away and eat your life up. Take time to renew yourself before God. Be brief and act quietly with your business affairs.

# TIME APART

If you give up all those things that provoke your curiosity and set your mind spinning, you will have more than enough time to spend with God and to attend to your business. Living your life prayerfully will make you clear-headed and calm no matter what happens. Your self-nature is overactive, impulsive, and always striving for something just outside your reach.

But God, working within your spirit, produces a calm and faithful heart that the world cannot touch. I really want you take an adequate amount of time to spend with God so that you might refresh your spirit. All your busyness surely drains you. Jesus took His disciples aside to be alone, and interrupted their most urgent business. Sometimes He would even leave people who had come from afar to see Him in order to come to His Father. I suggest the same to you. It is not enough to give out—you must learn to receive from God, too.

# IDLE IMAGINATIONS

You will sometimes carry into your prayer life a mind filled with idle imaginations and selfish thoughts. You will be torn between wanting to please God, and wanting to please yourself. Can you see how prayer can become so difficult and lifeless?

The very thing which could give you strength becomes powerless because there is so much inner struggle going on that your spirit is left unfed. How can you fix this? Lessen your distractions and spend more of your free time sitting before God.

I don't want to cut you off from your public duties. I don't think that you spend enough time visiting those you need to. But you really should re-evaluate what you do with your free hours. Indulge your curiosity less, and keep your business details to a minimum. Don't drag things out and learn the art of letting others help you. You tire yourself out more in studying disagreeable subjects than you would by visiting those who you think interfere with your free time. Take away your need to be distracted, and your need to always be busy, and you will find that all that is expected of you can quietly be done before God.

# THE FUTURE

Don't be so concerned about the future. The future belongs to God. He is in charge of all things and will take care of you completely. If you try to guess what is going to happen you will only worry yourself and anticipate trouble. Live each day as it comes. Each day brings its own good and evil, but what seems evil becomes good if you leave it in God's hands. Do not hold up His purpose by being impatient.

God has a time for everything. Never second-guess Him. One of the most important things you must do is live in the present moment. It is not how fast you go, but how well you go. God knows just how long it will take you to get from one place to another. You needn't always be rushing about. Simply follow God's leading.

All you need to do is prepare your heart by giving it completely over to God, without reservation. He will do with you what He pleases. Close your eyes and follow Him. Walk, as Abraham did, not knowing where you are going. God Himself will be your guide. He will lead you through the desert to the Promised Land. You will be so happy if you let God take full control of your life!

# TIME

How you spend your time changes with the different seasons of your life, but one principle applies to every moment of time: Don't waste it. Every season has various tasks that God has appointed for you to do and you will give an account to Him of how you have spent your time. God never wants you to look at any time in your life as purposeless. He doesn't want you to spend your time apart from Him.

The important thing to know is how God wants you to use your time. You will not learn this through hard work or schooling or a keen intellect, but by seeking God with a pure and upright heart. You also must put aside the schemes of your self-love just as soon as you notice them. For you do not only waste time by doing nothing or even by doing something you know is wrong; you also waste time when you do a seemingly "good" thing that God has not asked you to do.

You must continually depend on God's Spirit for His direction. If you have a doubt about what He wants, ask Him again. When the course becomes clear, move forward with His strength. Bring your heart back to Him whenever you feel yourself drifting away from God.

You are truly blessed if you leave yourself in your Savior's hands, willing to do whatever He wants. Never tire of asking God what He wants from you.

Meet each responsibility as it comes. God prepares you for them. The only thing you need to do is submit your temper, your opinions, your worries—your natural way of responding to things—completely to Him. Don't let yourself get overwhelmed by external business.

Seek, in every thing that you do, to glorify God. Do not get so personally involved with your duties that your whole thought life revolves around them. Don't let your work either excite you or depress you too much.

Time spent socially with others can be dangerous for you. You must learn to stay in the presence of God while you are with other people. There is a subtle poison often hidden in your conversation. Use your time with others to influence them toward God. Remember: Your words can do great good or great harm.

Spare time is pleasant. You can hardly find a better use for it than by renewing your strength through inward fellowship with God. You will learn the secret of spending intimate time with your Lord. Those who know the Lord well cannot resist turning to Him in every available moment.

# AMUSEMENTS

If you keep your heart set on God, innocent amusements are harmless. Being harsh, legalistic, and unbending will reinforce the false idea that serving God means living a dull, gloomy life.

Let the peace and joy of your life in God flow out for all to see. Even the most ordinary things, done in God's presence, are serving Him. God ordains even simple things to be done in His order and for His glory. Don't forget that!

Most people, in trying to please God, expect that God wants them to do difficult or unusual things. God wants you to die to yourself, and live to Him in the everyday events of life. Far more inward, rather than outward, changes need to be made in you if you lived a decent, moral life before your conversion.

God doesn't want your lip service—He wants you to let Him mold your will. Refuse Him nothing. Want nothing but His will. Seek Him during your hours of emptiness, and He will fill you with His grace. Even the most mindless pastimes can be offerings to God when you are expected, by family duty, to engage in them. How free you are when you do all things simply to the glory of God. Let God lead you by the hand without questioning Him. There is nothing simpler or more faithful than learning to accept the will of God apart from your personal taste—your likes and dislikes and impulses. If you live this way you will be easy-going, yet disciplined.

When your pastimes start to distract you from God, return to Him. When you are depressed or tired, bring your troubled spirit to your Father who holds out His arms to you. Look to Him when your emotions go up and down, and He will bring you into balance and never leave you without help. Look to Him, with a silent movement of the heart, and you will find new strength. Even if you feel discouraged, God will still give you strength to do what He expects of you. His strength is your daily bread—His strength is your very life. God does not forget His children. He waits to find your heart open so that He might pour the torrents of His grace out.

Have you ever seen a young child move happily from one place to another? Learn to be like this. Be happy to be tied down or to be free. When you cannot say anything worthwhile, say nothing just as cheerfully. I know that you always want to be occupied with serious matters. But God has not chosen this for you, and His taste is better than yours. It is good to not want to say silly or frivolous things, but God wants to take away the self-righteous satisfaction you feel toward always dealing with "important" matters. So He is going to disappoint you by letting you be involved with less serious situations.

You ask how you can keep yourself pure in a

lifestyle that is so public, and frankly, so shallow. First, read and pray. I am not being trite or shallow in suggesting this. And I do not mean reading to gain more knowledge. Nothing could be more vain! No, read some great word or deed of Jesus and ponder it in deep silence. Just be aware of the truth, and as your mind wanders away from it, bring yourself back to the present moment without being upset with yourself. You don't know how far this will get you.

Second, when you are free, take entire days just to withdraw and be alone with God. It is at the feet of Jesus that all the wounds of the heart are healed and all the soil of the world is wiped away.

Third, enter into your entertainments only as you are asked to do so. Be friendly, but do not seek out invitations. Those who watch you, at least the reasonable ones, will be happy to see you sociable enough to join them, but careful enough to not always be found entertaining yourself. And I take it for granted that when you do appear at these entertainments, you do so in a godly manner. The world is critical of people who condemn its ways, while living by its rules. This is the way it should be!

# WALK IN HIS PRESENCE

The heart of your life as a Christian is contained in God's words to Abraham, "Walk in My presence, and you will be perfect." God's presence calms your spirit, gives you restful sleep, and quiets your mind. But you must give yourself completely to Him.

It does not take much time to love God, to renew yourself in His presence and to adore Him in the depths of your heart. The kingdom of God is within you and nothing can disturb it.

When outward distractions and a wayward imagination hinder you from having a peaceful inner life, then you must, by an act of will, bring yourself before God. Not that you can force yourself into God's presence, but even the desire to come into God's presence is, in itself, a powerful aid to your spirit. Cultivate a pure and upright intention toward God.

From time to time you must stir up your deepest desires to be fully devoted to God. There need to be seasons when you think on Him alone, with a wholly undistracted love. Consecrate your senses to Him completely at these times. Don't get caught up with things that you know distract you both outwardly and inwardly from God. Once you are distracted from God it is hard to return to Him.

Whenever you notice that you want anything too much, then stop yourself immediately. God does not dwell in the midst of chaos and disorder. Don't get caught up with what is said and done around you. You will be deeply disturbed if you do. Find out what God expects from you in any given situation and stick strictly to doing that. This will help you keep your inner spirit as free and peaceful as possible. Get rid of everything that hinders you from turning easily to God.

An excellent way to maintain a quiet spirit is to let go of every action just as soon as you complete it. Don't keep thinking about what you have or haven't done! And don't blame yourself for forgetting something, or for doing something you regret. You will be much happier if you keep your mind only on the tasks at hand. Think of something only when it is time to think of it. God will tell you when the time comes to deal with something. You will exhaust your mind by trying to figure out God's will before the right time comes.

Make a habit of bringing your attention back to God on a regular basis. You will then be able to quiet all your inner commotion as soon as it starts to be churned up. Cut yourself off from every pleasure that does not come from God. Seek God within, and you will undoubtedly find Him with peace and joy. Be more occupied with God than anything else. Do everything with the awareness that you are acting before God and for His sake. At the sight of God's majesty, calmness and well-being should fill your spirit. A word from the Lord stilled the raging sea and a glance from Him to you, and from you to Him, will do the same for you.

Lift up your heart to God. He will purify, enlighten, and direct you. David said, "I have set the Lord always before me." Repeat His beautiful words, "Whom have I in heaven but You, and there is none on earth I desire that compares with You."

Do not wait for the time when you can shut the door without interruption. The moment you long for inward prayer is enough to bring you into God's presence. Turn toward God simply, trustfully, and with familiarity. Even in those moments you are most interrupted, you can turn toward your Father. Instead of being annoyed by unprofitable talk, you can find relief in finding a moment of inward fellowship with God. So you see how all things work together for good to those that love God.

Read what is suited to your current needs. Pause, as you read, to listen to God's voice directing you. Two or three simple words, full of God's spirit, are like food for the spirit. The words are forgotten, but they are still doing their work secretly, and the spirit feeds on them and grows strong.

# REST IN GOD

Virtue starts to grow in a heart that desires the will of God. It is not a question of knowing a lot, or being talented, or even of doing great deeds. All that you really need is to long to belong completely to God. But how does your will come to this place? By conforming little by little, but without reservation, to what God wants. You must learn to bring your weak will in line with God's all-powerful one. Here you will find inexhaustible and never-ending peace and joy.

Adore, praise, and bless God for everything! See Him in all things. There is no longer anything truly evil in your life for God uses even the most terrible sufferings to work for your good because you love Him. Can the troubles God uses to purify your life be called evil? Think of what these troubles accomplish in your life.

Rest all your cares on the bosom of the Father. Be content to follow His will in all things, and to let Him bring your will into harmony and oneness with Him. Do not resist Him as He works within you. If you feel resistance rising up inside of you, turn to Him and take His side against your own rebellious nature. He will know what to do. Learn not to grieve the Holy Spirit within you, for He watches over your inner life. Learn from the past mistakes you have made without getting discouraged.

How can you better glorify God than by renouncing your own desires and letting Him do what pleases Him? He is truly your God when you see nothing but the hand of God ruling over all things in your life, and you worship Him with no outside pressure and even with no inward comfort.

To want to serve God in some conditions, but not others, is to serve Him in your own way. But to put no limits on your submission to God is truly dying to yourself. This is how to worship God!

Open yourself to God without measure. Let His life flow through you like a torrent. Fear nothing on the road you are walking. God will lead you by the hand. Let your love for Him cast out the fear you feel for yourself.

# REAL PRAYER

Real prayer is nothing more than loving God. Prayer is not made great by a lot of words, for God knows your inmost feelings before you say them. True prayer comes from the spirit. You pray only for what you really desire. If you do not see what you are desiring from the depths of your heart, your prayer is deceitful. You could pass whole days "praying," but if you do not pray from your deepest, inmost desires, you are not praying.

You pray without ceasing when there is true love in your heart, and when there is a desire born of God there. Love, hidden in the depths of the spirit, prays constantly even when your mind needs to attend to something else. Love asks God to give you what you need and to regard your sincerity above your human weakness.

God's love within you removes even the slightest faults and purifies you like a consuming fire. The Spirit within you asks for all things according to the will of God. Even when you are busy with outward things there is still a constantly burning fire within you. This fire, which cannot be put out, encourages a secret prayer which is like a lamp always burning before the throne of God. "I sleep but my heart is awake."

There are two things that will help you keep this spirit of prayer: regular time set aside to be with God, and coming back to God as much as you can during the day. Stay away from people who distract you too much or who excite your passions!

The first fruit of a sincere love for God is the earnest desire to do all that you can to please your Beloved. To do any less is to love yourself before God. God forbid! Cost what it may, you must be willing to do all that He asks without reservation.

Do what you should before you go out to enjoy yourself. People who neglect their duties to "spend more time with God" deceive themselves. You won't get closer to God by being irresponsible and calling it "spiritual." Real union with God is to do all that is required of you by God, no matter what you feel.

Make sure you make time for God. Those who are in important positions are often busy and will be tempted to leave time for communion with God until last. Guess what? You will never have any time for God. Be firm with yourself. Don't let the confusion of the day crowd out your time with God. This may sound too strict, but you will soon fall apart if you don't listen to what I have to say about this.

# WANDERING THOUGHTS

How do you deal with wandering thoughts and lack of enthusiasm during prayer? Set aside a regular time to be alone with God. Just be content to yield yourself without reserve to God. Don't go out looking for the cross, but when the cross comes (and it will), do not let God's work pass without letting the trials become fruitful to you.

Accept, despite your natural reservations, all that God brings to you to exercise your faith. Don't worry about whether you will have the strength to do the right thing. Grace comes only in the moment that you need it. Just be willing to receive your trials with a cheerful heart.

When you see your thoughts wandering, call yourself back to the present moment, but do not struggle with your thoughts. Just stay in the present and you will soon notice your Lord by your side again. The more you turn back to Him just as soon as you sense yourself wandering, the sooner you will have the blessing of knowing the indwelling presence of Christ in a more constant and familiar way.

When you are completely given to God, all that you do is profitable, even if you don't do much. Offer your future up to God, and don't try to figure out what will happen to you. It shows your faithlessness when you want to know the future that God has chosen to conceal from all of us.

Leave the future to God. The best preparation is to die to self-will and give yourself wholly to God. Your spirit will grow as you become less weighed down by your self-nature. You get used to a life full of strife and endless labor and think this is normal. You will be surprised to see how simple and straightforward your life in God is.

It is enough to look to God with confidence, without trying to explain the past or reason out the future. If something distracts you from Him, then turn back to Him just as quickly as you can. You will make a lot of progress if you just keep turning back to God. This is much better than getting all upset about your faults and failures.

As for the depression that grows out of a melancholy personality, there are natural things that will help you—a good diet and exercise. You may have regular struggles with depression, like you would a headache, but it will pass. Your imagination sinks in deep despair, but the will, which lives by faith and not emotion, can pull you out. The question is not what you feel, but what you will.

If anything is capable of enlarging the spirit and freeing you, it is entire surrender to God. Nothing will keep your mind calm, content, and joyful as living like a child in the arms of God.

Christ wants you to follow the will of God and to live it out in the present moment. God has not designed His will to torture you or to overwhelm you in such a way that you always are looking at your performance.

When business keeps you from seeking God, then see Him working in you even then. See Him in all things. Always sing within you the songs of Zion—for the heavenly Zion is your true home. Speak simply, cheerfully, and trustfully, with the pure freedom which God gives to His children.

Never seek danger. Wait for the calm assurance that God will be your help and protection. Even the tasks that God has asked you to do should be continually surrounded with prayer and inward surrender. Never leave your place of inward rest until God Himself calls you out. Then He will go out with you, and while you seem to leave God, He will carry you in His bosom.

If God wants to use you to do His work with people, then yield to Him. Think not of yourself. Give back to God all that He has given you. However dangerous the calling is, just walk simply with God and do not look to yourself for strength. Your Father is good.

If God doesn't choose to use you in recognizable ways, do not force yourself into serving others. Peacefully do what stands before you. Desire or refuse nothing. Whether people seek you out or reject you, whether they applaud or oppose you, what does it matter? It is God, not the gifts of God and not yourself, that you seek.

Jesus says, "Learn of me for I am meek and lowly of heart, and you will find rest." Stay gentle and humble and you will know the peace and rest of God.

# WRONG DOING

When you realize that you are about to do something wrong, you must try to avoid it. But if you fail and do what is wrong anyway, then you must courageously bear the humiliation that you will feel. When you first sense the wrong before you do it, you must be careful not to resist the Spirit of God who is warning you of danger. If you ignore Him, He will grow quieter and quieter. If you continue on that wrong path, you will soon never hear Him speak at all. Your human weakness is nothing compared to deliberately becoming deaf to the voice of the Holy Spirit who speaks deep within you.

The faults you don't see until after you do them will not be cured by being upset about them. Quite the contrary. Your impatience with them is only your disgruntled pride witnessing its downfall. The only thing you can do is bear the humiliation your sins bring to you. It is not humble to resist being humbled. Be sorry for your faults, repent of them, make no excuses for them, but don't become bitter or discouraged over your imperfections.

Often what you want to give to God is not what He is asking you for. What He wants from you is what you love most. He wants the "Isaac" of your heart—the only son, the beloved. He wants you to yield up to Him all that you hold most dear. Until you do this you will have no rest. "Who is He that has resisted the Almighty and been at peace?" Do you want God to bless you? Give up everything to Him and He will be with you. What comfort, what freedom, what strength, what growth when self-love no longer stands between you and God.

Never be discouraged with yourself. It is not when you notice your faults that you are most wicked. You never really see your sins until they are beginning to be cured. Neither flatter yourself, nor be impatient with yourself. Despondency is not humility. Actually, despondency is the despair of your wounded pride. Your faults may be useful to you if they cure you of the vain confidence you have in yourself. God only lets you feel your weakness so that you may seek your strength in Him. Never act against the light within you. Follow God.

# SMALL THINGS

Great acts of virtue are rare because they are seldom called for. When the occasion for you to do something great comes, it has its own rewards: the excitement, the respect gained from others, and the pride that will accompany your ability to do such "great" things.

To do small things that are right continually, without being noticed, is much more important. These small acts attack your pride, your laziness, your self-centeredness, and your oversensitive nature. It is much more appealing to make great sacrifices to God, however hard they might be, so that you might do whatever you want with the small decisions of life. Faithfulness in the little things better proves your true love for God. It is the slow, plodding path rather than a passing fit of enthusiasm that matters.

Sometimes you cling to trifles more than truly important things. It would be more painful to give up one of your pastimes than to give a great deal of money to charity. You are more easily led astray by little things because they seem so innocent. Nevertheless, when God takes these little things away, you soon discover, through the pain of their absence, how attached you are to them.

Besides, if you neglect little things, you will constantly offend your family, the people who work for you, and everyone else! No one will believe you love God when your behavior is lax concerning small, important details. If you won't make small sacrifices, how will we believe you can make great ones?

You may need courage to attend to small things at first. It may not be easy. Accept the difficulty as God's discipline which will bring you peace. Things will get easier.

# DEPEND ON GOD

I know I talk a lot about being totally detached from yourself and about loving in a completely unselfish way. Since this is such a difficult thing to do, I don't want you to feel guilty when you fall short. Your failures don't make you displeasing to God. He sees your deepest feelings. It is a long process toward being completely dead to your selfishness. There will be self-seeking in many things that you do. You can tell if your old self is involved in a situation when something stands in the way of what you want and you are upset or disgruntled.

You cling to yourself without realizing it, but see how you cry when something is taken away! You do not deliberately hang onto your bad intentions, but you do not look at them too closely for fear of what you might find out! God reveals a thousand things in your heart which you will swear are not there, but He will help you deal with them.

Do you think you want to discover all your weaknesses at once? God tenderly spares you this frightening discovery. He does not send too much light too quickly. Do you see how admirable and good God is to not ask you to change something which He has not yet given you the resources to change?

The people who watch their faults the most are still in the dark about how to give up certain weaknesses. God reserves this wisdom for a more advanced state.

Be faithful to what God has given you—not to what He hasn't. God will show you, in His time, everything you need to know. Meanwhile, God hides your own imperfections behind a veil lest they overwhelm you. You impatiently want to be perfect, but it is much better to wait humbly under the hand of God. Bear with yourself without condemnation nor flattery. The process will work a deeper death to your self-nature than instant perfection.

God wants to foster your dependence on Him. He gives you light as a wise mother would give her child tasks to do. No more light is given until that particular job is finished. Have you finished all that God sets before you? He will instantly give you a new work for He never leaves you idle. But if you haven't done what He has asked, He will show you no more.

Let God work in you, and be happy with the light He gives you. Each new gift from God is built upon the one before it.

# PRIDEFUL FEELINGS

Whenever you see prideful feelings in yourself, or you feel that you know more than anyone else, or care for no one but yourself, then you must let all these attitudes drop like rocks in water.

Seek God and stop everything until you are calm and yielded to God once again. If business matters or your overactive imagination keep you from being quiet before God, then you must still bring yourself before God and want to be still. Wanting to be still and quiet before God is itself a prayer which strips you of self-will, and keeps you flexible in God's hands.

Don't congratulate yourself when you take a few steps toward God. The minute you are converted you think you know everything about God. You give up your major vices and are ready to be canonized as a saint. You are not judging yourself by the standard of the gospel, but by how you lived your past life.

In the long run this attitude will get you in more trouble than committing a blatant sin. A blatant sin would trouble your conscience. But thinking you are well, when you are really not, will stifle your spiritual life. Serving God is not just a matter of avoiding evil, but of learning good. So don't love

God a little bit and think that is all there is to it. You can't expect to live life as you please, then go to God as a last resort when you need help. Is this loving God? I think it is more like irritating Him!

To just read the Bible, attend church, and a-void "big" sins—is this passionate, whole-hearted love for God? You do not belong to yourself—you belong to God! You can't soften the gospel to adapt it your weakness. Woe to anyone who tries to widen the narrow way!

The only way to love God is to love Him completely. You have let everything else rule you—your emotions, the whims of others, your wayward desires. Plunge into God and give everything that you are to Him.

# SOCIAL RELATIONSHIPS

Allow your friends to come and go as they will. If someone says something to offend you, then put what they have said aside without brooding over it. As you expect less of others, you will learn to be kinder and more helpful to everyone.

How near we are to each other when we are all united to God! Aren't your relationships made easier when you have a single view to do the will of God? Do you want to find true friends then? Seek your friends only in God. He is the source of true and eternal friendship. Do you want to speak with and hear these friends? Then sink down in silence in the bosom of the One who is the very life of all those who speak and live the truth. In Him you will find every honorable desire met. In Him is perfection—compared with the imperfection you find in all relationships that are outside of Him.

You need to find a balance between totally withdrawing from social relationships, and spending all your time witnessing to others. You need to find a happy medium between taking care of your own needs and taking care of the needs of others.

You can work out this balance by considering several factors: Do you need to take time to renew your spirit? Are you healthy? How much time do you have? How does God seem to be leading? It is all right to consider the needs of the mind and body. Then see how you could best use your remaining time.

What good is it to stay with a person to whom you could be of no use, when there are others whom you could help? Of course, if you have an obligation to this person out of friendship or relationship then you should stay. Otherwise, treat that person honorably and be on your way. You don't have to make things hard on yourself in the name of the cross. If there is someone you don't enjoy entertaining then don't do so unless you are called upon to do so.

Do not withdraw or be sociable from self-centeredness. No doubt your self-interest will be mixed in with your decision, but simply do what you see is best. Because you have been so worn out, I think it best that you take as much time as you can to refresh yourself. Love more and suffer less.

# DEALING WITH TEMPTATION

Let's talk about the wrongs that you allow yourself to fall into. I am not talking about major sins—deliberate disobedience to God on major issues is not usually a problem a committed Christian deals with on a daily basis. I am talking about not stopping a sharp word, or being deliberately quarrelsome. These things you have some control over, but you let yourself do what you want.

The closer you get to God, the more miserable things you will find in your heart. This is not a negative thing—God allows it to let you lose confidence in yourself. You will have accomplished something when you can look at your inner corruptness without anxiety or discouragement and simply trust in God. But you should try to not let yourself fall into temptation.

There are two resources against temptation. One, be faithful to God within you. Avoid all that is better left avoided. Of course you are not always able to avoid these situations, some are brought to you by God and will do you no good to flee them.

The second resource is to turn to God when you are tempted. If you find that you've half consented to temptation, then head straight back to God. Take the example of a child who hides his face in his mother's bosom as soon as he sees something that frightens him.

Practice staying in God's presence so that you are able to respond to His leading immediately. In a way, there is little to do in doing the will of God. It is true that holding back nothing from God is doing quite a bit. God's love searches the secret places within, looking for anything that resists Him.

On the other hand, Christianity is not found in a multitude of rules, nor in holding yourself back from every pleasure. Just yield yourself to God without reserve. Live in the present moment. Let God do what He sees fit without resisting Him, and agree with God without trying to justify what you want to do. Temptation is a necessary part of a Christian's life. Don't be upset by even the most shameful temptation. Look at God and dwell continually in His presence—He will keep your feet from falling.

# THE PHARISEE AND THE TAX COLLECTOR

The Pharisees were religious reformers who carried out every detail of the Law. Their outward religion would dazzle you, but inside they were blinded by their own self-righteousness.

The tax collectors were social outcasts, hated by all. Jesus tells a story about the tax collector and the Pharisee. The tax collector is ashamed of his sin. The Pharisee is proud of his virtue. But God prefers the sinner, overwhelmed by his wretchedness, who trusts in God alone.

The Pharisee clings to the external trappings of God's gifts. He uses them to bolster his own righteousness. The Pharisee admires himself in the mirror of his self-love. But this one dirties himself every time he looks into the mirror.

The Pharisee is much more common than you think. Many Christians try to lead "good, Christian lives" and are proud of themselves for it. They may pray, tithe, and lead moral lives, but inside they are attached to their own ability to live the Christian life.

You have hidden (or not so hidden) pride at your own strength. You take pleasure in seeing yourself as strong and good and righteous. But whom are you trusting, and whom are you looking at in all of this? Yourself! You want to know the good feeling that comes with being right with God. You need to empty yourself, not fill yourself up. Follow God by the dim torch of faith, not by the light of your own understanding and abilities. Do not be proud of your apparent ability to live the Christian life. Your ability to do that will soon prove to be an illusion. Trust in God alone.

# TRUE FAITH

Do you realize that you are not walking by faith when you need to know that you are doing well? Constant evaluation is just a preoccupation with yourself. Is this centering on the Lord Jesus Christ? When you feel yourself getting distracted, turn to God. Do you see that constant introspection is, itself, a distraction? You seek comfort in self-reflection, and in the defense that it brings to your ego. You are afraid to pray poorly, but you pray best when you don't even realize you are praying. You want to feel supported and assured in the way you practice your faith—true faith is walking without that support. Remind yourself of Jesus crying out on the cross, "My God, My God, why have you abandoned me?" God withdrew His presence from Jesus and it was the last blow for the Man of Sorrows. Live by faith.

# THE FALL OF MAN

You really don't understand how far man has fallen if you expect any good from him. Stand in awe that the new stem of Jesus Christ bears good fruit within you. Discount all human acts of virtue—they are poisoned with smugness and self-confidence. There is an inward idolatry that is worse than outrageous outward sins. Let God humble you. There are all sorts of hindrances to those who seek God. You can't go as fast as you want because your faults stop you. Your pride, and all the baggage that it carries, slows you down. Sometimes you think you are moving right along, but you cheat here and there to keep up appearances. At worst you think you really have abandoned everything when your selfishness is very much intact. That is probably the worst thing of all.

And then you start to turn and judge others. You start to mistrust the people you are secretly jealous of. Jealousy, hidden in your deepest inner folds, exaggerates the least faults of others. Then come the disguised criticisms. You deceive yourself in order to justify yourself. God may disturb you out of your selfishness for awhile, but slowly you drift back toward your own interests.

This is what horrifies me. I beg God to deal a complete death to this selfish nature of mine or I will live a life full of selfish misery. I may look more spiritual than most people, but inside God sees the hypocrisy. It must make God sick, but when will it make me sick enough to submit entirely to God?

When you start talking about Christianity in this light, when you speak of total abandon, people accuse you of being fanatical and unbalanced. This is because they don't want to completely die to their own desires. Your self interest hides in a million clever disguises. There is no end to the excuses we will come up with. This struggle is in all of us, even those whose hearts are toward God, because our will is still weak.

Even your outrage at the faults of others is a great fault. Don't you see your own wretchedness? It would certainly level your self-righteousness to the ground. All mankind, including you, is corrupt, but don't be discouraged. God is preparing His true servants. They have faults, but God is at work in them.

# HELP FOR DISCOURAGEMENT AND DEPRESSION

You get discouraged because your mind wanders too much? What do you expect? Theresa of Avila says, "The imagination is the fool of the house." It concocts wild scenarios and takes you away from being aware of God in the present moment.

Go forward. Stop listening to all the horror stories your imagination whispers to you. Go forward. You feel sad because you look for God and do not feel His presence as much as you want. You tire of trusting God by faith. You tire of hanging in the air. You want to see progress! You make one mistake and fall into a depression. What pride! What self-obsession!

Love God and stay still before Him. You would rather punish yourself, and stir up a commotion, than forget yourself and look to God. Mourning your weakness will not make you better. It will only contribute to a good case of self-pity. The slightest glance toward God will calm you far more.

As far as a natural depression that comes from physical reasons, simply endure it in peace. Set your eyes on God. Do what He shows you to do. If He has need of you, fine. If He does not, then live before Him in peace.

As for being disappointed in others, you must learn not to expect so much from people. It is the only way to avoid disappointment. You must take the fruit that a tree bears—but remember that some trees only put out leaves and caterpillars! God has an infinite amount of patience with you, as He does with all people. He is not even put off by their resistance to Him. Try to imitate His patience and mercy. Only imperfection is bothered by the imperfect. The more mature you grow as a Christian the more patient you will be toward the faults of others.

When depression weighs you down, there are two things that might help you. First, relieve your sadness with the means that God gives you. Don't overload yourself with difficult things. Guard your strength of mind as well as your strength of body. Don't take more upon yourself than your courage can bear. Set aside time for being with God, for reading, and for good conversation. Take time for harmless entertainment which will relax the mind with the body.

Secondly, bear in peace all the feelings of sadness which still remain with you after you have done all these things to help yourself. Don't fight with them and they will go away in due time.

# THE DANGER OF
# FRIENDSHIPS

It is natural to want to have a good friend whom you admire and like. It is a great pleasure in life to have friends, but friendships can be full of danger, especially if you live in community with a close circle of people.

As a member of the Body of Christ, you no longer belong to yourself. In a group that meets to honor the Lord Jesus, you must guard against forming special friendships. These will lead to cliques or a party spirit. Sometimes, when someone you like has been hurt, you become emotionally involved and "pick up their offense." This will cause division in a house faster than anything I know. You are soon plotting and chatting in secret and a sense of divisiveness permeates the entire affair. Of course you appear to yourself without blame, and insist you are only standing up for what is right.

Others watching this are harmed. You set a bad example for them and usually force them, in a subtle way, to take sides. On top of this I just want to tell you that jealousy comes between two people who are devoted to the same friend. Each fears the other will be preferred. And what problems this causes!

Furthermore, when you have a special or favorite friend, it puts that person in a difficult spot. A person who is loved by another often makes the whole community jealous or critical. They either want to enter into a special friendship also, or are critical for what they think that person to be. Often there is suspicion and misjudgment. Everyone is caught up in looking at someone other than Jesus. Finally, you harm yourself. You can become so preoccupied with others that you lose sight of the lordship of Jesus in your life. You spend less time alone with Him. You think of your friends and neglect your Lord. And as you say, "I can handle this relationship," watch out!

Try not to single people out to love them. Love equally all those God asks you to love. If you know you are preoccupied with a friendship, try to cure yourself little by little. See all people as they are—with their good and bad points. Then you will not romanticize them. What is your self-nature getting out of these unhealthy attachments? This is something you ought to look at. Love your friends in and for God, and not for what they give you. Don't be so selfish.

# FORGETTING YOURSELF

To forget yourself does not mean to forget to thank God for His gifts. Nor does it mean that you never think of anything that has to do with you. It means that you do not make yourself the center of your world. When you forget yourself, you no longer deliberately seek everything for yourself.

A poor peasant, who has never been outside of his village, only partially knows how poor he is. But take him to a palace and he will begin to get a perspective on his state! So it is with you and God. You can hear all sorts of sermons about the vanity of riches, etc., but it does not sink in until God Himself shines His light into your spirit. Then you will see how far apart you are from Him in character!

Although your goal is to love God purely for Himself, and for His sake alone, you have to realize that in this life it is almost impossible to love God with total unselfishness. God has to do that miraculous work in you, and it takes a long time.

He will give you a purer love as you go along, but that is up to Him.

# DIFFERENT CALLINGS

Do you prefer to see God's gifts working in you rather than in others? This is self-attachment! Do you think I exaggerate the lengths God will go to strip you of your selfishness? He will pursue you relentlessly until you are completely pure. Nothing is as jealous, as severe, and as sensitive as His pure love. What an ordinary person sees as necessary to have, God will take away from a person He is purifying.

But I want you to realize that God does not pursue everyone this way in life. There are many believers whom He leaves in some degree of self-interest. The blessings and gifts that God gives to them comfort them. It would be dangerous to take these comforts away from them. Such people glorify God for His goodness. They gain from what God gives them and they thank Him for it. But some are called to go beyond this point and seek God's glory alone, as Jesus did. You must never look down at someone who is not called to walk the way you are. God does what He wants with each one. Do not desire to escape if God calls you further, and do not inquire to know more if He doesn't.

# THE SCHEMES OF
# SELF-LOVE

Do you really think you are generous and look out for your friends more than yourself? You want to see yourself as an unselfish person who sacrificially loves others. This kind of thinking will slowly poison you because it lets you believe that you are doing better than those weak people who are still living for themselves. You don't seek to use your friends, but you hope they will be charmed by what you do for them. Of course they will tell you that you are wonderful and have no self-love, and what could be sweeter to your self-love than being praised for not having any?

Your self-love has only become more clever and refined. Stop kidding yourself! Do you want to unmask it? Criticize it!

Your self-love wants to be esteemed by spiritual people. You want to seem interesting and unselfish, but of course you can't let yourself think this openly. As you fool others, you fool yourself. You begin to believe the illusion you create.

Only God can help you. I know you have many questions. It is easy to see the need of giving up things that are obviously wrong, but how hard it is to give up things that people see as good—honest wealth, a prosperous lifestyle, or a good reputation. Now these things are not evil, but your relationship with them must be severely dealt with. A good steward only uses what he needs. A Christian must renounce everything so that it will not destroy him.

You must renounce those you love best—your family and your friends—and be ready to lose them if God takes them away. Never try to find your heart's true rest in them or you will experience the jealousy of God. God rejects a bride who divides herself between Bridegroom and stranger.

Worldly people find it hard to renounce their body: They are worried about their looks, and about growing old and wrinkled. But Christians can become proud of renouncing their bodies and making sacrifices!

When you see yourself going your own way, and being impatient with others, then return to God and sit still before Him with a lowly heart. If you make a mistake, go forward. Your pride doesn't like to make mistakes. The grief and embarrassment you feel from your mistakes will serve you well. Always follow God's leading. When He gives the signal, risk everything to follow Him. Nothing is so terrible as resisting God within. If you grieve the Holy Spirit, where will that leave you, my friend? God will draw back from you and leave you to your own way. And you, spinning around in circles, might not notice it for a long time.

God has given you simplicity and straightforwardness. Let Him build on this foundation.

# SIMPLICITY

To be simple is a marvelous virtue. By simple I do not mean intellectually slow or retarded in emotion, but straightforward and unhindered before God. Simplicity is hard to define, but as the *Imitation of Christ* says, "It is better to practice it than to know how to define it."

Simplicity cuts away all useless behavior. Sincerity is not the same thing. There are lots of people who are sincere without being simple. They speak only what they feel to be true, but they are always studying everything and weighing words against each other. People are not at ease with them, and they are not at ease with people. There is nothing free, easy, or spontaneous about them. Imperfect people who are less regimented are preferable to strict and legalistic souls. This is how we look at it, and God, I think, looks at it the same way.

The people of the world are too much preoccupied with each other. But the self-righteous religious person is too much preoccupied with himself. One is drunk with the external. The other is drunk with the internal.

Simplicity cuts a balanced path through the middle of all this. A truly simple person starts to consider himself less and God more. God wants you to look to Him naturally without anxiety or reservation. Surrender to God little by little and simplicity will grow in your spirit.

You must also allow your restless attitudes to be dealt with. Even your eagerness to serve God must be dealt with. I hope this thought will help you to calm down without becoming totally passive. Your overeagerness mars even the good things you do and sets you at odds with the peaceful spirit of God. Ask God to make you simple.

As to how you should dress, you should consider your husband's opinion. If he doesn't want you to spend a lot of money because of family debts, then you should be economical in your taste. If he wants you to appear fashionably dressed, then do so within reason. If he has no preference, then I would suggest moderation because you are so prone to extremes. Dressing magnificently only appeals to your pride. But dressing too conservatively and primly can also appeal to your religious pride. Dressing in an ordinary way helps you to feel ordinary. I am told that you used to dress like a nun. This was too much appearance and too little reality! Moderate dress will cost your pride a good price.

# THE FOUNDATION OF HUMILITY

Everyone who has deeply walked with God knows that humility is the foundation that you build your spiritual life on. True humility comes from seeking the interests of God before your own. Humility comes in no longer living for yourself but in letting Jesus Christ live His life in you.

You are always trying to "be something" or to be noticed for your spirituality. There are a lot of people who have an outward spirituality, but inwardly they still think too much of themselves. People who think they are lowering themselves have a lot of conceit. They think they are doing others a favor in "getting down to their level."

True humility is not like this. I know it sounds incredible but a truly humble person is content in all situations. He doesn't notice if he is being praised or blamed, and isn't always weighing if what is being said to him, or about him, is to his advantage. A simple person allows himself to be led by the Lord Jesus. So let go of yourself with courage. Whether God lifts you up or lets you remain unknown, the glory is still all His. Say, as Mary did, "He has done great things because He has regarded my low estate."

# Part III

## The Peace of God

# THE PATH OF FAITH

Don't worry about the future—worry quenches the work of grace within you. When God gives you comfort, enjoy it. Look at Him continually. Enjoy His provision day by day as the Israelites received their manna. Do not try to store anything. There are two peculiar things about the walk of faith. Faith discerns God behind all the circumstances that try to hide Him. Faith also holds you in a state of uncertainty. I want you to realize how continually you will feel suspended in the air and not allowed to walk on solid ground. The comfort you find in this moment will be completely inadequate for the next.

Let God act in your life in whatever way He chooses. All you must do is to be faithful to what He asks of you. God wants you to depend on him from moment to moment. The darkness and uncertainty of your life's path must bring you to rest peacefully in Him. To trust Him even when you do not see where He is taking you is a true death. It is a silent death that happens without fanfare.

Dying to yourself will feel like a slow fire. The end comes so quietly and inwardly that it is often hidden just as much from you as it is from those who know what you are going through. When God takes things from you, He knows how and when to replace them. He can then give them back to you Himself or through others. He can raise up children from stones.

So eat your daily bread without thinking of tomorrow—"sufficient unto the day is the evil thereof." (Matthew 6:34) Tomorrow will take care of itself. The One who feeds you today is the same One who will feed you tomorrow. Manna will fall from heaven in the middle of the desert before the children of God will want any good thing.

# REMAIN AT PEACE

I am not surprised to hear that your impressions of death become clearer as you grow older and weaker. I experience the same thing. There is an age when you begin to think about death more frequently—even irresistibly. God makes use of this to let you feel your own weakness and lack of courage, and to keep you humbly in His hands.

Nothing is more humbling than an imagination that runs out of control. Once the imagination starts to spin it is very difficult to have confidence in God. Here is the crucible of humiliation, where your heart is purified by a sense of weakness and unworthiness. In His sight no man is justified. (Psalm 143:20)

Continue to walk humbly with God without interruption. If you are shown something that should be corrected, then simply do so without becoming legalistic about it.

Remain at peace. Do not listen to the voice of self-love, or mourn the impending doom of your self-nature. Offer yourself, without complaint, as a sacrifice to God. St. Ambrose was asked, when he was dying, if he was afraid of God's judgment. "We have a good master," he said. Bear this in mind.

Can you see that you need to die in the deep uncertainty that you really do not completely see yourself or know your character as God does? You do not know exactly what God will say to you until you stand before Him. Augustine has said that you need to have nothing to give to God but your wretchedness and His mercy. Your wretchedness is what His mercy is for. In your deepest hour of sadness, read whatever will strengthen your confidence in God. Pray for a clean heart. No doubt He will pour out His compassion on your failings.

# INWARD PEACE

I want you to find inward peace. Peace cannot be found except with a lowly heart. And a lowly heart is not something that you can conjure up. Meekness of heart is a gift from God every time you experience it. The perfect time to experience a humble heart is when someone disapproves of you, or when you experience inward temptations and weakness. Learn to get used to both of these trials: They are a part of life.

You can make progress toward lowliness when you are no longer surprised when someone has to correct you and you do not want to be corrected. You may even see that the correction is right but you are unable or unwilling to correct the wrong. This leads to despair and depression because you then do not expect God to help you.

Sometimes scoldings, even harsh ones, seem to be less than you deserve. And when you do not receive them cheerfully, you condemn yourself for being too sensitive. But your sensitivity points out that there is still something alive within you that has not died to self.

I am sorry if I have spoken too harshly to you. Do not doubt my affection for you. Count as nothing everything I say to you. See the hand of

God which makes use of my awkwardness to deal you a painful blow. The pain proves that I have touched a sore spot. Yield to God and His dealings and you will soon be at rest within. You give this advice to others; take it yourself. What grace will fall upon you if you embrace all the situations that God uses to humiliate you and cut you off from yourself. I pray that He will so diminish you that you can no longer be found at all!

# LIVE IN LIFE

Nothing makes me happier than seeing you peaceful and simple. Isn't it like paradise? I know you don't have any great pleasures, and you do suffer some pain. Thank God you don't need the former, and the latter you receive with a grateful heart.

Inward harmony, which has grown out of the death of self-love, produces a joy greater than any earthly delight. Live in your earthly paradise and do not be tempted to leave it to experience good and evil.

You are never alone when you are in the presence of a single, faithful friend. You are never deserted when God carries you in His almighty arms. All comfort comes through God, and is not added to or subtracted from by the channel He uses. And should this comfort break forth from within your own heart, you have no need of any other created person. How can you feel regret that the voices of the Old Testament prophets have stopped when you are able to hear God's voice within your own spirit?

# TRUE PEACE

You want to be perfect. Is that the only way you can find peace? Real peace comes when you see your own faults, faults neither hidden nor tolerated, and completely admit that you are wrong. When you do this you will learn to accept how frail and weak you are. You will have made progress toward trusting God simply because you no longer trust yourself.

God's peace will only be found when you set your self-seeking aside. When all you desire is God's glory and His will, you will know peace as deep as an ocean. Nothing can disturb that peace except holding back a part of your heart in fear. Being indecisive will cause you all sorts of trouble. Your mind will try to spin you around in circles.

Your faults may bother you more than the faults of others because God requires that you sacrifice yourself in order to deal with them. Be faithful to the light that God gives you. You have a history of being too legalistic, and your unrealistic standards will overwhelm you if you don't watch out. Just do what God shows you to do— nothing more.

By all means do not try to raise doubts within yourself through constant questioning. If you have a real doubt, bring it to God. If God requires something of you, then obey Him. If He shows you something He is going to require of you, then use that insight to prepare for the sacrifice rather than to fret over it. Follow God in peace and ignore all the arguments your mind sets up. Resign yourself to God and do the best you can.

In the moment that nothing matters to you except God's will, you will find every hindrance cast aside. Throw away your earthly ideas and you will spare yourself much grief.

# INWARD SILENCE

God is your true friend and will always give you the counsel and comfort you need. Do not resist Him! Learn to listen to Him in silence so that you won't miss a word of what He says to you. You know a lot about outward silence, but little about inward silence. You must practice quieting your restless imagination. Stop listening to your unrenewed mind and the kind of logic it has! Get used to coming to God and asking Him for help when He asks you for something you are afraid to give.

Your sensitivity to the smallest affairs shows how much you need God to tear the things of the world from you. You are making great progress when you begin to give God all the childish attitudes you have, and let him deal with the "small" problems of your life. You need not make a deep show of spirituality—just let God work on your everyday issues. You can die to yourself in the course of your everyday life—you don't need to go out into the desert, or on some high mountain to be spiritual. All God asks of you is to give Him what He directs you to. To do this you must watch and pray. Cultivate trust in God—not your vanity or curiosity or lazy nature.

# SEE GOD IN ALL THINGS

Love others in and for God. Often you love yourself, reflected in another. Is this the love of God? No, it is self-love, and not real friendship. How do you love your friends? Love God in them. Love what God has deposited in them. When you love your friends for what they can do for you, you will soon be impatient, jealous, and mistrustful. You will expect perfection and find only disappointment.

But God's love in you knows how to love patiently and does not find fault with people. His love within you will cause you to be thankful for what is of God in your friends. You will not be impatient about what is lacking in your friends. All that is good comes from God. Submit to His plan in your life, and be glad about what He gives you in His mercy and love.

God's love never expects to find you perfect outside of Him. God alone is perfect. Learn to see Him at work in others and be thankful for that. See that God's love can be reflected in the love a parent has for a child. In every human relationship you can find something to learn about how God loves you. God is strict about His feelings toward marriage. This is to preserve the strength and intimacy of man and wife, for marriage is an important symbol of your relationship with God.

Can you love God and not love those He has asked you to love? Can He not supply you with the love you need to obey Him? God's love in you endures all things, bears all things, hopes all good things for others. His love can conquer all obstacles as it flows out from within your spirit.

Love is touched with compassion for the sorrow of others, but causes you to think nothing of your own. God's love comforts, weeps, rejoices, encourages all in perfect time. Let your heart overflow with genuine love—not a cold, forced imitation. Learn to let God within you spring forth from within your spirit. Nothing is so sterile and cold as someone who only loves himself. There is nothing to compare to the tender and lovely gentleness that God's love produces in a human heart.

# SAY YES TO GOD

Becoming perfect is not becoming boring and strict like you think. What it demands is that you should be totally devoted to God from the depths of your heart. When you are totally given to Him, then all that you do for Him becomes easy. Those who are completely God's are always content because they want only what God wants. In giving up things that displease God, you will find yourself a hundred times happier. You will know a clear conscience, a free heart, the sweetness of surrender to God, and the joy of seeing the light increase in your spirit. On top of this you will be delivered from the harsh dictatorship of your fears and from the evil desires of the world.

You may give up things, but it is for Him whom you love best. You may suffer but you will still be upheld deep within. And you will say a continued "yes" to all that God needs to do to conform you to His image.

God only wants one will between the two of you. Let yourself become soft in His hands. Are you afraid to give up your will to God? How blessed you will be to throw yourself into the arms of the "Father of mercies and the God of all comfort." What a mistake to fear giving yourself too completely to God. It only means that you are afraid of being too happy, of finding too much comfort in God's love, of bearing the Cross in your life too bravely!

Let go of the things of the earth so that you might belong completely to God. You need not give up everything entirely. When you already live a life before God, balanced with discipline, all you need is to let God's love direct and motivate you from within.

After your conversion, your position in life may not change although you will! Serve God in the place He has put you. So instead of being eaten up with pride and passion, you will live with freedom, courage, and hope. You will find that you can trust God, and you will look forward to eternity, making your current trials easier to bear. When earthly happiness slips away from you, God's love will give you wings to fly into His bosom, above all your troubles and cares.

# ABSOLUTE SURRENDER

Inward peace comes with absolute surrender to the will of God. You need to come to a simple calmness of spirit which comes from giving up everything to God and having patience with your neighbor. Learn to accept counsel with humility and straightforwardness. This will help you grow closer to God.

The reason you feel so agitated is that you do not accept everything that happens to you with complete trust in God. Put everything in His hand, and offer yourself to Him as a sacrifice. The moment you stop wanting things to be your way, you will be free from so much worry and concern. You won't have to hide anything or make up excuses for anything.

Until you reach this point of surrender, your life will be full of trouble and aggravation. Your talents will torment you. Your religious ideals will condemn you. So give your heart wholly to God and you will find peace and joy in the Holy Spirit.

# PRAYER OF SURRENDER

My God, I want to give myself to you. Give me the courage to do this. My spirit within me sighs after you. Strengthen my will. Take me. If I don't have the strength to give You everything, then draw me by the sweetness of Your love. Lord, who do I belong to, if not to You? What a horror to belong to myself and to my passions! Help me to find all my happiness in You, for there is no happiness outside of You.

Why am I afraid to break out of my chains? Do the things of this world mean more to me than You? Am I afraid to give myself to You? What a mistake! It is not even I who would give myself to You, but You who would give Yourself to me. Take my heart.

What joy it is to be with You, to be quiet so that I might hear Your voice! Feed me and teach me out of Your depths. Oh God, You only make me love You. Why should I fear to give You everything and draw close to You? To be left to the world is more frightening than this! Your mercy can overcome any obstacle. I am unworthy of You, but I can become a miracle of Your grace.

# ONE THING NEEDED

There is never peace in resisting God. "Martha, Martha, you are troubled and uneasy about many things. Only one thing is needed." (Luke 10:41-42) The one thing is to trust completely in God in a childlike way. Something happens and you are upset. You are easily shaken away from your confidence in God. Do you think God is not in control? Do you think He does not care? The less you have to hold onto, the happier you will be. Your mind, in holding onto its thoughts and reasoning, will torment you. If you can't see past men to God, you will encounter much turmoil.

Know that God loves you. He runs like a shepherd who tires himself out to find his strayed lamb. He Himself obeyed God to His death. Rest in God's hands.

The future is God's. Live with God in the present moment. Live your daily life out in the presence of God. He will give you all that you need.

# YOU ARE MADE FOR GOD

Everything is for God, and for His purpose. Of course He wants you to be happy, but that is not His highest aim. God's glory and His purpose are the end of all things. So seek out the eternal purpose of God and get in line with it. You will find happiness and salvation there, but not as an end in itself. It is all for God.

Not many people can even think of being all for God, and not for themselves, but this is the highest calling. It is hard to hear or understand this because you want to live for your own interests. And it is hard to convince a modern person that God is his final end, and that everything in life should be to God and for God. This doesn't mean that you can't enjoy yourself and your freedom in God. You must simply want God's purpose fulfilled more than anything else in creation. You belong to God, you have been made for Him. Your natural instincts tell you to protect your life, and take care of yourself. There is nothing wrong with this, but you can live by a deeper instinct within your spirit that lives only for God's glory.

Some people love God because in His goodness He reaches out to save them. But you can experience love for God even if He never reached out to save you (although this is an impossible supposition!). You can love God simply for who He is, and not for what He does for you. Do you see the difference? It is not wrong to be glad that God has saved you, it is simply better to not dwell on that, and to live for what God is really after in redeeming you.

If you think this kind of love is impossible, I have two things to say. Nothing is impossible with God. Are you going to accuse the greatest Christians of every generation to be living an illusion simply because you cannot match their standard?

Secondly, eternal life is a gift of God's grace. He is not obligated to give it to you, but He, nonetheless, has given His Son for you to inherit it. If, just for example, He chose to not give me eternal life, if at the moment of my physical death I disappeared into oblivion, then God and His purpose have not changed, have they? God was never obligated to save me, was He? Everything I have from Him, my life itself, is a gift of grace. Even if He chose to not save me for eternity, He is still my Creator, and is free to do with me what He wishes. God is still God. His character is still the same. His purpose remains unchanged. Shall I not still love Him for this?

But God has prepared you to be His forever. Dare you love Him too much? I will still love Him no matter what He does with me. Dare you love Him less, when He loves you more? Will the reward that awaits you make you more selfish? Is eternal life your goal, and not God Himself? Your love is weak indeed if this is true!

# KNOWING GOD

Most people don't really know God. They know what they have read, or been told, but it is an intellectual knowledge that lacks true spiritual experience. Most of us grow up being told there is a God, but I'm not sure how much we believe it. We don't act like we believe in God. And those who believe in God have a relationship based on fear rather than love.

How many love God and want to know Him for Himself? I pray there will always be such people even if they are rare. All of us were made for God. But when people are told to seek God within, it is like telling them to go to another planet. What is farther away and more unknown than the bottom of your own heart?

Oh God, we don't understand You. We don't know that we exist through You. Help me to see You everywhere. You allow an amazing thing: a mixture of good and evil in the hearts of even those who are most given to You. These weaknesses keep us humble and close to You. So choke back in my heart all that rises up to question Your goodness. Let me sit in silence before You, and then I will begin to understand. Nothing presses You to overwhelm Your enemies. "You are pa-

tient," says Augustine, "because You are eternal."
Oh God, love Yourself in me. The more I love
You, the more You pursue me with Your relentless
love. Oh God, I adore You. You have made me for
Yourself alone. I exist for You.

# LOVE GOD
# WHOLEHEARTEDLY

Dwell in peace. Your feelings of devotion to God and your enthusiasm to serve Him do not depend on your own ability. The only thing that you can control at all is your will. Give God your will without reservation. The important question is not "Do I enjoy being a Christian?" but rather, "Do I want what God wants?" Confess your faults. Do not be too attached to things of this world. Trust God. Love Him more than yourself. Love His glory more than your life. If you do not want these things, ask to want them. God will come to you with His love, and put His peace in your heart.

# Library of Spiritual Classics

This is volume four of our ongoing series of books made up of great spiritual classics of the past which we are modernizing and republishing. Thank you for your constant encouragement that urges us on. If you would like to be placed on a list of people receiving announcements of all new releases in this series–as well as all books we publish on the deeper Christian experiences–please write us.

Volume five is an incredible little book entitled *The Spiritual Guide* by Michael Molinos. Included in it will be a short biography of that unusual and controversial man.

## SeedSowers
P.O. Box 3317
Jacksonville, FL 32206
800-228-2665

904-598-3456 (fax)   www.seedsowers.com

# THE CHRONICLES OF THE DOOR *(Edwards)*

- The Beginning ................................................................. 8.99
- The Escape ...................................................................... 8.99
- The Birth ......................................................................... 8.99
- The Triumph .................................................................... 8.99
- The Return ....................................................................... 8.99

# THE WORKS OF T. AUSTIN-SPARKS

- The Centrality of Jesus Christ ........................................ 19.95
- The House of God ............................................................ 29.95
- Ministry ........................................................................... 29.95
- Service ............................................................................. 19.95

# COMFORT AND HEALING

- A Tale of Three Kings *(Edwards)* ................................. 8.99
- The Prisoner in the Third Cell *(Edwards)* ..................... 5.99
- Letters to a Devastated Christian *(Edwards)* ................ 5.95
- Healing for those who have been Crucified by Christians *(Edwards)* ........... 8.95
- Dear Lillian *(Edwards)* .................................................. 5.95

# OTHER BOOKS ON CHURCH LIFE

- Climb the Highest Mountain *(Edwards)* ........................ 9.95
- The Torch of the Testimony *(Kennedy)* .......................... 14.95
- The Passing of the Torch *(Chen)* .................................... 9.95
- Going to Church in the First Century *(Banks)* ............... 5.95
- When the Church was Young *(Loosley)* ........................... 14.95
- Church Unity *(Litzman, Nee, Edwards)* ......................... 14.95
- Let's Return to Christian Unity *(Kurosaki)* ................... 14.95

# CHRISTIAN LIVING

- Final Steps in Christian Maturity *(Guyon)* .................... 12.95
- Turkeys and Eagles *(Lord)* .............................................. 8.95
- Beholding and Becoming *(Coulter)* ................................ 8.95
- Life's Ultimate Privilege *(Fromke)* ................................ 7.00
- Unto Full Stature *(Fromke)* ............................................ 7.00
- All and Only *(Kilpatrick)* ................................................ 7.95
- Adoration *(Kilpatrick)* .................................................... 8.95
- Release of the Spirit *(Nee)* ............................................. 5.00
- Bone of His Bone *(Huegel)* ............................................. 8.95
- Christ as All in All *(Haller)* ............................................ 9.95

\* call for a free catalog 800-228-2665